Glowglass

Books are to be returned on or before
the last date below.

Published by
Strident Publishing Ltd
22 Strathwhillan Drive
The Orchard
Hairmyres
East Kilbride
G75 8GT

Tel: +44 (0)1355 220588
info@stridentpublishing.co.uk
www.stridentpublishing.co.uk

Published by Strident Publishing, 2018
Text ©Kirkland Ciccone, 2018
Cover art & design by Andrew Forteath
www.andrewforteath.co.uk
Cover image via www.doctormacro.com

A catalogue record for this book is available from the British Library.

ISBN 978-1-910829-25-7

Typeset in Garamond by Andrew Forteath | Printed by Bell & Bain

VHS or Betamax?

1

Video Venom

Hello.

Is this recording? Give me a few seconds to get started.

If I spin around fast with this camcorder, I can pretend we're in a hurricane.

Whooooosh!

Ugh. I feel dizzy.

Do I look better from this side…or this side?

Actually, I look like a depressed trifle from that side.

This side is much better.

Okay. Are you ready?

By the time you watch this, I'll be long gone.

But where do I start?

TCR 00:00:15:23

At the beginning, I suppose. What *is* the beginning? Is it the morning we all ate breakfast together for the last time? My first day in Morvern High? No. That won't work. That won't work at all!

It *has* to be the last breakfast first and everything else afterwards.

SIGH

Here we go. Are you sitting comfortably?

You won't be for much longer.

TCR 00:00:18:57

Breakfast made me an orphan when I was fifteen years old. And do you know what I discovered that morning? I realised for the first time that revenge is **not** a dish best served cold. It must simmer in a large pot of milk before being served piping hot to twenty-five people. And despite how it ended, everything started normally that day. My brothers and sisters enjoyed routine, all of us choosing a table in which to receive The First Daily Blessing, which came in the form of breakfast.

Since there were lots of us, we usually took ten minutes to get settled.

We said nothing as *he* tipped salt into each and every bowl of oatmeal.

Salt in our bowls, salt in our wounds.

It was his favourite form of petty malice, wasn't it?

If you wanted sugar, he gave you salt.

If you wanted love, he gave you hate.

I often tell people that breakfast killed my family, but I'm only half-serious.

Only two of us survived that day.

Me and you. You and me.

Free, free, free from the whole family.

One moment our brothers and sisters were eating, the next they were dead.

And when I looked over at you, sitting at the other side of the largest table...

You didn't look surprised.

Not in the slightest.

Because you knew there was something else in the oatmeal that morning.

2

Vocab Test

Our lives were never normal. You know it. I know it.

Why deny it?

But what *is* 'normal' anyway?

'Normal' is something invented by Kellogg's to sell boxes of *Corn Flakes* to housewives.

It's a myth, just like gods and monsters.

Actually…there are such things as monsters.

I'm the daughter of a monster.

You know that better than anyone.

And if anyone else watches this video, they'll know too.

TCR 00:00:25:47

Whenever I look back at everything in my life – and I've been looking back a lot in recent days and nights – I finally see how messed-up we were when *he* was alive. Do you think it's possible for a person to be unhappy if they don't know what it is to be happy?

I often stared at the four walls and dreamed of what lay behind them.

Did you realise we were trapped?

Did you know that our home, our church, was also our prison?

TCR 00:00:26:03

As long as I can remember, and probably as long as you've been alive, this old place has been called as The Sanctum. Who came up with that anyway? Maybe it was Father. It certainly sounds like the sort of fancy label he'd put together. *Sanctum* is very ostentatious, isn't it? It's much better than The Old Dump or

The Rotted Mansion.

By the way, just to let you know…I scored high on the vocab test a few weeks ago with the word *ostentatious*, which is why I've just used it. *Ostentatious* means 'designed to impress'. Weirdly, I think it suits the crumbling old mansion we've spent our lives living in…no, wait, *living* is the wrong word. You and I know that we only started to *live* after he died. *That*'s when The Sanctum became our own little world away from the people behind the four walls, hidden at the edge of the town, on the fringes of everything.

The Sanctum is so old that no-one can remember it being new.

History sticks to things, doesn't it?

The Sanctum would never be home, just a place we lived, if only for a while.

I'm so tired of lying. I know you feel the same way.

That's why I'm recording this for you.

It's a message.

Or a prayer.

You decide.

3

Religious Education

In the beginning there was Sorak The Almighty. Sorak, an omnipotent being, was also very bored. If you think about it, omnipotence probably is very boring. Isn't mortality what makes time precious?

Omnipotence is also another word from a Vocab Test, but I already knew what it meant anyway. Just in case you don't, an *omnipotent* being is someone or something with unlimited power.

And if you were lonely and had limitless power, what would you do?

You'd create a world, of course.

That's what Sorak did in the beginning when there was nothing but a void.

He made the world and everything on it.

He made the people, plants, trees, sky, and seas.

He made the stars so we could tell the time.

He made language so we could speak.

And what did we do when we learned to speak?

We communicated. We created. We continued His great work.

And then we messed it all up.

You see – and I've only just realised it – Sorak The Almighty may have given us all these nice things…but He also gave us war, hatred, racism, disease, and violence.

Maybe there's some greater perspective that small people like you and me can't see. But I tried. I honestly did. I just can't see why anyone would want to create this world. Why inflict so much misery on some people while the other half don't see or care?

Perhaps life is His joke on the world?

Sorak only knows.

4

Father

You've often told me that no-one is born evil, but you're wrong. *He* was born evil. That's why he did all of the things he did. And that's why *we* did all of the things we did. I don't feel bad about what happened…well, there is one thing I feel bad about, but I'll talk about that soon enough. I once said, "I'm brave enough for the both of us," – do you remember? I wasn't lying, but I'm not being entirely honest either.

One thing frightens me more than anything else in the world:

The truth.

TCR 00:00:32:23

5
Tell It

I used to play a game when I was a kid. I'd sneak downstairs where no-one other than Father was allowed to be, and I'd pretend to be different things. I'd shapeshift into furniture and stay hidden from view. If I wanted to be a lamp, I'd stand very straight and tall. If I needed to become a table, I'd get on my hands and knees and pretend to be made of wood. Why was I so uncool? Perhaps my subconscious was prodding me to blend in and fade into the background? Once, while trying to be a hat stand with no hats on me, I discovered something scratched into the wall beside the little brown Formica table at the far end of the hall, to the left of the locked red door.

My reading wasn't good at that age, but I translated the words, breaking them down slowly until I could make sense of them. I read aloud, but still didn't understand:

Her name was Noelle until they changed it.

When I asked Father what it meant, he didn't get angry. How could he? I was his favourite. But He explained that before he bought the estate, it used to be a place where young unmarried girls were sent to give up their children. But he assured me that the glory of Sorak The Almighty had cleansed the surrounding land of all negative energies.

I accepted because I had no choice.

But it didn't make sense.

There's no good in this place.

6

What's In A Name?

People beyond the four walls of the estate had no idea he was so evil. Let's be honest, they still don't know the truth about him. He never once showed them his true face. The mask never slipped. As far as everyone else was concerned, he was a kindly old man with a big heart, a big family, and a bigger bank balance.

He was a big hypocrite too.

We were his Children, his wonderful happy Family.

He was Deacon Randolph William Glowglass or *Father*, as he preferred us to call him.

There are other names I'd like to call him, quite frankly.

TCR 00:00:57:46

7

I Am Little Star

What sort of a name is Deacon Randolph William Glowglass anyway?

Actually, what sort of a name is Starrsha?

My name, obviously. You already know it.

But other people will probably see this tape and watch me tell my story.

So, I dedicate this next bit to them:

TCR 00:01:00:05

I'm Starrsha Glowglass. I'm fifteen years old and I've been brought up to believe that the finger of Sorak is pointed at me, prodding me towards great things.

I was Father's favourite, his star pupil. That's why he called me Starrsha.

"Little star," he used to whisper in my ear late at night, as the moonlight peeked through the curtain crack.

In hindsight, it would have been nice to have had curtains that fitted my bedroom windows.

8

The Holy Words

Things changed after he died. Mostly for the better, but we aren't lucky enough for *that* to last. It started to go wrong for us that one day you went into town with a smile...and returned with a frown. I didn't pay attention at first, but I realised at dinner something wasn't quite right. You kept turning the same lettuce leaf over time and time again.

"What's wrong?" I asked.

You wouldn't lie to me. You've always tried to live by Sorak's Commandments, and didn't He write this in Volume Two of *The Iconic Black Books of Sorak The Almighty*:

Lies of any kind are stains on the soul.

You replied to me in the only way you could.

Your fingers blurred into action, making letters, forming words:

I GOT A LETTER FROM THE LAWYER ASKING TO SEE ME.

That's when you reached under the table.

You thrust your hand into a small cloth satchel.

And pulled out the video tape.

TCR 00:1:05:51

9

Plastic Shell Held Together By Five Screws

It was just like *him* to use a museum exhibit to terrorise us from beyond the grave. He had only been dead for a few weeks, along with the rest of The Family, and yet we still had to put up with his shenanigans. He always made me feel utterly helpless. Scumbag.

"What are we supposed to do with that?" I asked, shrinking away from the cassette in your hand. I studied it with probing eyes before deciding it looked like every other videotape I'd ever seen in my life:

It was black rectangular plastic: 187mm wide, 103mm deep, 25mm thick.

It may as well have been a bomb, given the impact it was going to have on us both.

His handwriting was on the side of the tape, scribbled on a white label.

Again, your fingers moved to make sentences:

THE LAWYER SAID WE HAD TO WATCH IT.

Your expression held a trace of anger, despite your effort to hide it from me. You've always tried your hardest to keep calm, and we both know you hate getting angry.

Because when you get angry, your face reminds me of his face.

Why couldn't we forget the past and find a better future?

WE BETTER GO DOWNSTAIRS AND SET UP THE TV, you told me.

"I have better things to do," I declared factiously. But that wasn't strictly true, because all I had was a book I'd tried to read and failed to finish it each time. In that moment, that very second, I panicked and considered pretending to be sick. Bouts of sudden illness weren't unusual for me – they seemed to happen when I was about to do something I didn't want to do…like watching whatever was on that damn tape.

11

10

Marlene Dietrich

Father always had a passionate love of old Hollywood glamour and beauty. How could someone so ugly be such a lover of beautiful actresses? Would you laugh if I said Father cared more about Marlene Dietrich than he did either of us? No. You'd probably agree with me. If faced with the choice between spending money on some food and beds for his Family, or some rare black and white movie from the fifties, then he'd choose Marlene. I suppose it's just as well we made plenty of money from the oatmeal processing plant. Without that money, we'd have nothing but grain.

As for Marlene Dietrich, I like her even though she has the word *die* in her surname.

Isn't that strange?

Father watched all his movies in his personal cinema, which was downstairs, in the hallway just up from the forbidden locked red door that haunted my dreams.

His cinema had a VCR machine to play his favourite tapes.

TCR 00:1:10:28

11

The Secret Cinema

It was the only place in the house we could watch the tape. You're sitting in it right now watching me on this tape, aren't you?

But on that particular day, we went straight downstairs to the special room, which wasn't nearly as special as we thought. It was a small man-cave with photographs of strangers on the wall, women posing with smiles, and men preening with attitude. Publicity shots, I later discovered, of Hollywood movie stars; Jimmy Cagney, Bette Davis, Joan Crawford, Marilyn Monroe, Henry Fonda, Miriam Hopkins, Clark Gable, Jimmy Stewart, Humphrey Bogart, Mae West, Clara Bow, Louise Brooks... They meant nothing to me. Why would I care? I'd never watched a movie in my life. None of us were allowed to watch movies – in case our thoughts were polluted with impure ideas! But Father clearly didn't mind watching them in private. Raging old fraud.

We found a rack of videotapes neatly arranged on a steel rack bolted to the wall. There was also a television – old-fashioned bulky, with a second skin of dust. After you flicked the switch and filled the TV with voltage, the spicy scent of hot wires and burning plastic reeked out the room.

You covered your nose and pulled a face, just like me. I laughed, didn't I? I had to do something to break the oppressive atmosphere.

Father's cinema had remained untouched during the intervening weeks. (*Intervening* is another word from a vocab test.) The last people in this room had been the police during their investigation into all the deaths. I can't tell you how much I wanted to tear down all those posters. But no, they're still there... glamourous wallpaper in a dirty old room full of videos. If you look away from this screen, you'll see them now.

The place is a museum dedicated to another time, an era of glamour and lies.

We looked at each other, united in uncertainty.

DO YOU WANT TO PUT THIS IN THE MACHINE?

Gingerly, with trembling fingers, I pushed the cassette tape into the VCR machine.

And then his face invaded the screen.

TCR 00:2:15:59

12

Children Of Sorak

"Children of Sorak," Deacon Randolph William Glowglass announced grandly from the screen in front of us, "I am gratified to see you again!"

His eyes blazed with insanity – the thin shield between dedication and delusion.

Why did we allow that idiot to control us?

You reacted oddly to the sight of Father. This was only weeks after you'd argued with him upstairs in the study. You never did tell me what that was all about, but I think I know now. Anyway, I watched you watching him on the screen; you sat straight up with your fist on your heart, an automatic response, the result of years and years of brainwashing. The worst part of seeing you regress was that it made me realise I too had my fist clenched across my heart.

It was so sudden I didn't even realise I was doing it.

TCR 00:02:24:13

We sat in silence and waited for Father to speak from beyond the grave, the videotape our equivalent of a spirit board, and the VCR remote control our glass over which we searched for meaning in the voice of the dead.

Father smiled warmly. I felt sick as he talked.

"If you're all watching this special message, then it means one thing. I have won my battle to pass the Golden Gates of Heaven, where Sorak has been waiting to greet me."

He quietened whilst apparently contemplating something important.

"This also means I've been murdered."

The cup in your hand exploded, spraying the carpet with a mixture of milk and blood. It upset me to see you in pain, even when you tried to hide it. But I kept that to myself. I've kept *so much* to myself. Hmm. What did I say to you after you broke the cup?

"I'll clean it up," I said, making sure you hadn't sliced open an artery.

"*Yes,*" Father's voice floated dreamily from the TV, "*I've been murdered. The visions were accurate. A few weeks ago, I was told by Sorak that I'd die quickly and suddenly.*"

TCR 00:02:31:08

Isn't it funny how Sorak only gifted The Deacon with these visions, all of which were beneficial to him and decidedly negative for everyone else? But this time Sorak was quite wrong. There was absolutely nothing quick or sudden about Father's death. He choked and spat up the contents of his belly, as did all of our brothers and sisters.

"You're going to bleed to death and I'll be the only one left," I scolded you while trying to stem the flow of blood. With your uninjured hand, you took the remote control and pressed <PAUSE> as I headed upstairs to find a bucket of water and a wet cloth.

Why did you bring that stupid tape back home? Couldn't you have just dumped it in a bin somewhere? Why did we have to watch it? We could have been happy here if you hadn't brought him back into our lives.

But you did.

And that's why I'm here on the screen in front of you right now.

That's why I'm covered in blood.

Don't worry. It isn't mine.

13

Sorak's Special Gift

"The foreknowledge of my impending death sits oddly with me."

Father suddenly didn't seem quite so insane, which was ridiculous because he was talking about premonitions of death on a videotape he'd recorded before he died. But in those few shots of video footage...he didn't look like the head of our Church, nor a businessman in charge of the oatmeal production line. Instead he resembled a frightened old man. Isn't it fascinating that he knew the end was coming to him? How could he possibly have predicted his death? *Maybe*, a small voice inside my brain told me, *maybe everything he told you was true and everyone else in the entire world is wrong.*

Rationality won out against delusion. It was a constant battle against my inner voice.

You were keen to know what else Father had to say, so you leaned close to the screen, carefully watching his lips so you could understand the message.

"It was while praying in solitude that I had a strong feeling someone would kill me in my own home, in front of my Children. I begged Sorak for guidance and this morning as I oversaw the sifting process of the oatmeal..."

I laughed out loud.

You looked across at me, whilst pressing a bandage against your hand.

"He never oversaw the sifting process," I seethed. "It involved cleaning the oats and he regarded cleaning as something for women and girls, not work for *men* like him."

Then I added, "If you could call that a man."

You smiled, but it wasn't a real smile. I always know the difference between real smiles and fake smiles. I'm an expert at fake smiles, because I've used them my entire life.

I took the remote control and rewound the footage. It had the effect of speeding Father's face backwards, which was funny. Well I thought it was funny. I uttered another laugh, then pressed PLAY and listened to what he had to say. Again.

"It was while praying in solitude that I had a strong feeling someone would kill me in my own home, in front of my Children. I begged Sorak for guidance and this morning, as I oversaw the sifting process of the oatmeal, he blessed me with a vision."

We watched together as Father's face twisted on the screen, his gently persuasive voice slowly changing to accommodate his other voice; the one he used during sermons.

I'd almost forgotten the sound of his ranting.

"Sorak told me that I would be betrayed by one of my own Children."

His next comments were spat out as short sentences.

"Traitors are not required in our happy home!"

"Traitors are not welcome in our happy home!"

"If I am to die here in my happy home, then it means one of you killed me!"

"It only became a happy home when you died," I shouted defiantly at the screen.

HE CAN'T HEAR YOU, you signed with a bandaged hand.

I knew he couldn't hear me, but it felt good to shout at him knowing he couldn't answer back. The best thing about talking to a TV screen is that it's passive and won't respond to insult…just like Father's poor wives after they married him.

We sat and waited for the inevitable. It felt like we were rushing towards some great but unknowable disaster. But what else could we do? We're all powerless against fate.

Everything that had happened had *had* to happen.

"I have sent this videotape to my lawyer and instructed him to keep it safe until the time comes for you to claim my money. You will not be hearing my Last Will and Testament."

Father paused, trying to create a tense moment worthy of a scene from one of his favourite old movies. He probably heard a dramatic orchestral score in his head.

"Yet."

An eerily familiar feeling of dread rippled through me.

"If my lawyer has done as I instructed, then everything is happening according

to the sacred instructions of our saviour. *Blessed be those who follow Sorak The Almighty!"*

We sat in silence, waiting for the video to end. It took another minute for The Deacon to wrap up his rather erratic eulogy before we finally arrived at the real reason for this stupid message. This was the reason for your meeting with the lawyer.

Father, it turned out, had set a trap in a tape.

"You will soon receive visitors," he said smugly from the safety of the TV.

We both leaped out of our chairs at the same time:

"What?" I cried.

But he wasn't quite finished.

Even in death he enjoyed the sound of his melodious voice.

"I have made preparations in anticipation of my execution. Everyone in the Church will not forget me quickly. All of you will finally understand that there is life after death."

That should have been the end of the tape, but something horrifying happened.

Father turned around on the screen *and looked right at me.*

Slowly, I backed away. The sickening feeling of fear returned – a fear I thought had died along with him. It wasn't possible. How could he know where I was sitting? How could he look out of a TV screen and see me as I was during that day?

"I'll always be with you. Forever and ever and ever," he said with a horrible smile.

Then you ejected the cassette and stamped on it until it bled black tape.

14

Teenage Girl Crush

It wasn't until everybody died that I first went to school. Education wasn't given freely because The Deacon knew fine well that education meant knowledge – and knowledge meant power. He didn't want to share power or spark anything even close to curiosity. Too dangerous. But I was his Little Star, which meant that I was allowed private lessons.

Everything I needed to know came from a tutor, one of the rare strangers allowed into the hallowed Sanctum of Glowglass. Whenever someone from the outside breached the four walls, we looked on in amazement. Initiates to our Family were commonplace, but visitors? They were like the Loch Ness Monster: you had to see them to believe them.

Father ensured I was taught everything that was required of me as a girl of the Church, which of course meant I knew virtually nothing useful or practical. He always sat in on my lessons, his eyes piercing and penetrating. He wanted to make sure I said nothing blasphemous about Sorak and didn't discover anything about the world beyond the walls.

He didn't like it when I daydreamed. He controlled everything, even my thoughts and hopes and fears and dreams. He was Sorak's messenger and his message was one of terror.

TCR 00:04:44:15

Do you remember Miss Gibson? She was my first crush. My first and only private tutor. She was the most exotic creature I'd ever seen in my life. She always wore a large red flower in her black hair, a burst of striking colour. Her skirts were so short, so immoderate, that they almost showed off her knees! If I ever wore anything like that…well, you know what would have happened. And if you can't remember, then let me quote something from one of *The Iconic Black*

Books of Sorak The Almighty:

The higher the hem, the lower the standard.

My education, though limited, saved me from a childhood of mind-numbing boredom. I'd been starved of knowledge and Miss Gibson was keen to fatten my brain. One useful thing she taught me was sign-language, which meant I could speak to you and even better...you could speak to me.

TCR 00:04:59:58

"You're very good at this," she said one day as we sat in the kitchen, our books opened at various pages. I glowed with pride. She thought I was good at something!

"She needs no praise," Father said, widening the distance between us.

I'll never forget the look Miss Gibson gave me after he said what he said. It took me years to understand it, until the day I looked in the mirror and saw Miss Gibson's expression all over my face: it was *sadness*. Miss Gibson felt sorry for me.

When Father died, you were the first to tell me to get out and go to school. And that's exactly what I did.

15

The School Of Tomorrow
For The Teens Of Today

My first day at Morvern High School was one of the singularly most terrifying experiences of my life, but it had to happen. For as long as I could remember, I'd dreamed of leaping over the four walls. Turns out I didn't need to leap. I just had to walk out the front door knowing that Father wouldn't be able to drag me back by the hair. I'd prepared everything in my head for weeks, committing to a new lifestyle, one that didn't revolve around ritual and prayer and goddamn oatmeal. I'd staged many rehearsals in my head as to how my first day at school would go. Nothing would go wrong. Everything had been reviewed in my fantasies: what I'd say, what they'd say back, and what I'd do.

But I had to get my new wardrobe sorted! With some money from our emergency bank account, we went shopping for clothes, so I could dress like everybody else my age. Do you remember my reaction when I saw a staircase moving by itself? We found it in the mall, a glitzy place that overpowered my eyes and ears with colour and noise. You held my hand and smiled reassuringly, but fear made me weak and sick. Where did those stairs go? What did they do? Why were they moving on their own? Did they ever stop?

But it wasn't a staircase at all, of course.

It was an *escalator*. I'd freaked out over an escalator.

TCR 00:05:01:49

An escalator will prove significant later on in my story, but you know that don't you?

EVERYTHING WILL BE FINE, you said with frantic fingers, THERE ARE MANY MIRACLES OUTSIDE THE FOUR WALLS OF THE

SANCTUM.

You meant well and I pretended to find your comment funny. (Miracles? Really?) But you were wrong to assume everything would be fine. Remember when I returned from my first day at Morvern High and told you that I'd had a brilliant day?

Oh, I laid it on thick, like sweet strawberry jam on one of our oatcakes.

"I had lots of fun and made friends for life!"

But I lied. They were never my friends.

TCR 00:05:18:12

Here's how my first day at Morvern High unfolded:

I arrived far too early and got lost in the labyrinth of corridors and staircases. My body rebelled against me, my legs quaking constantly. To compensate, I greeted every single person I passed in the corridors with a cheery "Hello, I'm Starrsha." Eagerness isn't a worthy value amongst teens at school. They all looked at me the same way Father looked at everyone else. Perhaps I've judged my classmates harshly, but Morvern High is my only comparison. I can only tell you what I know – and I know my classmates don't see education as something to improve their lot in life: they regard it as a necessary evil at best, or a five-year survival course at worst.

One girl (whose name I don't know) literally screamed as soon as her eyes fell on me.

The comments and jibes were just as loud.

I heard each and every one of them.

I *felt* each and every one of them.

"Is that a tourist or something?"

"She looks stoned."

"I think she's the oatmeal girl from that creepy old townhouse in the hills."

"Shhh. She watched her family die."

"Her shoes make *me* want to die."

"I don't think she's wearing a bra!"

That's when I made a terrible mistake.

I asked a question.

23

The wrong question.

"What's a bra?"

The girls in the corridor couldn't believe it and reacted with screeching laughter.

Father always said it didn't do well for anyone to ask questions. He said that asking questions led down the path towards the fury of Sorak.

On my first day at Morvern High, I found myself agreeing with him.

Now you can't blame yourself for my misfortune and embarrassment. How were you meant to know I'd be such an idiot? It wasn't like I could ask you about bras and tampons. There *were* others behind the four walls that could have guided me. Milly, for one, would have helped. Mary-Beth or possibly even Joannie too.

But they were in Heaven with Sorak The Almighty.

All of them left us after eating bowls of poisoned porridge.

TCR 00:06:07:55

16
Shared Facilities

Deacon Randolph William Glowglass – dear old dead old Dad – had many rules that we had to abide by while we lived under his roof. Each rule was backed by a quotation from *The Iconic Black Books of Sorak The Almighty*, and there were over twenty iconic books, all of them bound in black leather. If you wanted a quote, he could give you one. If you didn't want a quote, you'd get one anyway. There were quotes for every conceivable situation that life could throw at the unwary disciple.

On my first day at Morvern High, one quote in particular resonated in my head. It can be found in Volume Three of *The Iconic Black Books of Sorak The Almighty*.

And the quote?

If at first you don't succeed, just give up. It isn't worth the hassle.

But I didn't want to give up and quit school on my first day, even though I felt like it. You taught me about perseverance. The world working against you, yet you've learned to live in it. If you were in my position, you'd keep going with your head held high. I'd fought too hard to get to Morvern High, to a place where I could be accepted. Father was gone, so being at Morvern was an act of defiance against his wishes. And that made all the initial misery worthwhile.

I never told you about my first day at school because I didn't want to leave. Giving up would have been like surrendering to Father, granting his wish. And that will never ever happen again.

TCR 00:06:57:36

Everything about Morvern High School was different to anything I'd ever experienced. It is a modern, sleek, beautifully-designed building with doors that open by themselves. This time I didn't freak out. But...I mean...doors that move without being pushed! Isn't that amazing? The rest of the school is similarly modern. The colour scheme is white and purple. The corridors are painted with white and purple stripes. The lockers – big metal boxes for our bags – are painted in a bright purple coating. They are the same colour as blueberries, which aren't blue despite their name. Blueberries are definitely purple. The toilets at Morvern High are for boys *and* girls. That didn't bother me too much though. Anything is better than our old toilet in the hut outside, so cold during winter that it froze into a thick block of yellow ice. In the summer, bugs and beasties hide in the rim, waiting to pop up!

The school toilet might not have insects and cobwebs, but it has something else: graffiti.

Most of what I've read on that wall isn't anatomically possible, though I haven't tried it.

I swear.

17
Bad Habits

Everything is here in my head, deposited for future reference. I've always been good at remembering stuff. That's why I can tell you everything that happened on my first day at school. If this isn't photographic memory, it's probably Post-Traumatic Stress Disorder.

Mr Dalmuir, the terminally sad-looking headmaster of Morvern High, introduced me to my classmates, the wonderful students of Room 4D. That's where English is taught.

Mr Dalmuir reminded me of the old Deacon, because of the hairy nostrils.

Does that sound bitchy?

I reckon I've picked up some bad habits along the way.

Here's what happened as I remember it:

TCR 00:07:44:11

Mr Dalmuir silenced the entire room with a clap of his hands (similar to Father again, funnily enough) and motioned at me with a gnarled finger – the sort that had been curled around a pen for far too long.

"I'd like to introduce everyone to our newest student," he said, his voice like dust blowing in the breeze. Don't think I'm being flowery with that description. I know the sound of dust in the breeze, because I scattered the ashes of twenty members of our Family during a monsoon. The way they fluttered in the wind, that dry sound, is virtually identical to Mr Dalmuir when he lets loose that voice in front of his students.

"Hello," I said brightly to my new classmates, "I'm Starrsha Glowglass. I'm fifteen and I like parties, music and going out at the weekend with my friends."

I'd never actually been to a party, hadn't been allowed to listen to music for most of my life, and didn't go out during the week, let alone the weekend. But there was a need in me...maybe a weakness...to try and please people. Why? Because I wanted to belong to something that wasn't a cult or a Church or whatever people said I was part of.

When you first suggested I leave The Sanctum to be with people just like me, you failed to understand one vital fact:

There *is* no-one like me.

18

"Dan"

Things got a little bit better two weeks after my first day at Morvern High. I'd made a conscious effort not to dress less like a member of our congregation and more like the girls in my classes. Out went the dungarees and plain shoes; in came a bright array of colourful fabrics. It wasn't difficult to copy my classmates. But once again my efforts to blend in failed. For some reason, they didn't seem to like it when I came to school wearing the exact same clothes they all wore. They seemed offended that I dressed in their style.

The worst was a girl named Olivia Gilfeather, an absolute pest in pink.

"Can't you get some originality?" Olivia screeched when I showed her my new pink blazer. I'd seen her wearing it, so I bought the same jacket to show her I had good taste too. Actually, the blazer was a cheap tacky mess – the sort of thing Father would have ripped off my shoulders had he still been alive. He would then have tied me to the post outside the garden and forced me to recite some choice quotes from *The Iconic Black Books of Sorak The Almighty*.

TCR 00:08:01:44

Actually, that happened to you once, didn't it?

What did you do to upset him?

Why did he make us spit on you, one at a time, all of us, until you were dripping?

I suppose I'll never know.

TCR 00:08:15:02

No. Don't wander. I have too much to get through and this videotape won't last forever. The timer at the bottom of the screen...those funny numbers,

TCR whatever. They're spinning faster and faster and faster away from me, sooner and sooner and sooner, nearer and nearer and nearer until the tape stops recording. And then it's all over.

TCR 00:09:11:57

Okay. Where was I? Yes! I know. I was telling you all about my time at Morvern High. It wasn't all depressing. Things got better for me at school two weeks into my curriculum. I made my first new friend. Dan. She's a girl with a boy's name, which is unusual because according to Volume Two of *The Iconic Black Books of Sorak The Almighty*:

> *A girl with a boy's name is a mistake to be corrected.*
> *A boy with a girl's name is a problem to be solved.*

Normally I would have stayed clear of a girl with a boy's name, but ever since I'd decided to live my life without the tedious finger-waving of Father, this rule suddenly seemed very silly. After all, why would Sorak The Almighty have a problem with someone's name? Does He really have so little to do that names would bother Him?

TCR 00:10:01:54

Dan was tall and thin with short brown hair. Her face was pretty but, unlike the other girls, she wore no make-up. But her face didn't need too much colour anyway, not with her eyes which glittered bright green. She wore a shapeless black hooded top with something written on the front: GERARD WAY. I sat alone in the canteen, eating a packed lunch full of fruit and nuts. She came over and sat at the table across from me. She smiled a beautiful smile, before her hands tore the wrapper from a small bar of oatmeal.

TCR 00:11:02:43

Have I already told you this story? I think I did; only I left out the bit about the oatmeal bar. She had a small bar of oatmeal and didn't seem to understand why I was so freaked out. How could she have known? She was just eating her lunch.

"Hello," she said softly, "you're new, aren't you?"

"Yes. I'm Starrsha Glowglass. I'm fifteen and I **hate** parties, music and going out at the weekend."

The girl laughed. It was a delightful sound that I didn't hear often enough. The only time we were allowed to laugh was when Father gave us permission.

"My name is Dan," the girl said, offering her hand across the table.

"That's a boy's name," I replied lightly. If my lack of sophistication fazed her, she didn't show it. If anything, I knew what it was like to not quite fit into the right space in life.

"It's short for Danielle, but all my friends call me Dan."

"I like it," I said, hoping that Sorak The Almighty wouldn't be angry with me.

TCR 00:11:56:14

My eyes looked at the oatmeal breakfast bar in her hand.

I shivered.

She didn't notice.

"Starrsha is such a cool name. Do I call you Starrsha or Star?"

"Starrsha," I replied with a contorted grin on my face. Cool? Really?

"Do you know what everyone is calling you?"

Yes. The front page of every newspaper in the country called me by the same name.

"The Oatmeal Girl," I replied, looking down at my lunch.

"I've always liked oatmeal," Dan said, "so I think we should be friends."

And just like that we became friends.

19

Adolescent Hearts

In the days that followed, Dan became my guide to the world outside the four walls. The problem with everyone in the world is that they see the world with spoiled eyes. But for me, everything was exciting. My heart soared at the sight of things most people took for granted. Alongside my new best friend, I explored different places in town. My heart no longer felt heavy, the way it had since our Family had died. I felt free enough to be me, whoever that was at that point. It didn't matter. I wanted to find me.

Dan took me to the carnival. Oh, the carnival! Tangy smells filled my nostrils, until my belly responded with an excited growl. The lights and noise were bright and loud, a party for everybody to enjoy. Cotton candy (or "candy floss", according to the nice lady who served me) tasted like a sweet cloud. I also ate a whole hot dog to myself, but not before checking whether or not it was made from an actual dog. It wasn't, thank goodness.

I drove my first dodgem car thanks to Dan.

"But I don't have a driving license," I told her.

Dan laughed until she realised I was being utterly serious.

"It isn't a real car," she said while pushing me into a bright red cart.

A few minutes later and we were crashing into each other in our little cars.

Then we went to the cinema and watched movies about superheroes who could soar over skyscrapers in a single leap. We ate more hot dogs, slathered in red sweet sauce that didn't taste of tomato regardless of what the label on the bottle read.

Hot dogs are my new favourite food. They're better than oatmeal with salt.

"Let's go to Boomania," Dan cried out as she pulled me past lots of different shops.

TCR 00:12:31:28

Boomania is a record shop that sells old junk. It also sells videotapes. Movies from the '80s that Father would have turned his nose up at, the way he did at everything he disliked. But the best thing about Boomania is a wall covered in rows of neatly arranged black vinyl discs. Something about them caught my magpie eye. Vinyl, according to Dan, is what old people used to listen to music. They were like videotape, except vinyl has endured whereas video cassettes are relics that don't belong anymore.

Just like us.

TCR 00:12:48:43

We kept returning to Boomania, even though it smelled like a toilet, just so we could listen to bands with weird names like BRATMOBILE, EMILY'S SASSY LIME, HOLE, SKINNY GIRL DIET, MY CHEMICAL ROMANCE, SKATING POLLY, THE JESUS AND MARY CHAIN, NIRVANA and lots more.

My head, brain and body couldn't get enough of all those new experiences.

Then we hit Pizzamania, a little hut with a fancy candy-coloured roof and posters of Italian men on the walls. Or at least I thought they were Italian. Dan told me that Pizzamania was actually owned by a Polish couple. I nodded, though I had no idea what she meant. That's my default setting: nod and smile if you don't understand anything.

"This is nearly as tasty as a hot dog," I said as I bit into a floppy piece of three-cheese pizza, the hot red filling sticking to my lips, dripping onto the wooden board on the table. The drinks were soft drinks, which fizzed my taste buds into a frenzy, a good feeling, and I guzzled the lot in one sitting.

"I love pizza too!" Dan said sincerely.

"I want to marry pizza," I told her, just as sincerely.

Then:

"Is it true?" Dan suddenly asked me.

"That I want to marry pizza?" I replied in amusement.

Dan snorted up some fizzy cola, such was the strength of her laughter.

"No, I mean is it true what people say about you?"

Honestly, I had no idea what people said about me other than that I was clueless about bras and designer labels. And I'd worked hard to change all that anyway.

What *had* Dan heard about me? Did I even want to know?

"I heard you were raised in a cult," she said in a low voice.

"I grew up in a big old mansion built on the edge of a field. We processed oats in the largest barn, while the smaller barn was where we held our sermons."

I explained to Dan that we weren't 'a' family.

We were *The* Family. The Family Glowglass, to be exact.

Brothers and Sisters. Fathers and Mothers. Secrets and lies.

We know all about secrets and lies.

I keep secrets. You tell lies.

20

Dan's Funny Moods

Dan had already started dropping hints about visiting me at The Sanctum, but I chose to ignore her out of respect for you and our departed Family. Despite these heavy-handed attempts at breaching the four walls, I still enjoyed spending time with Dan, even when she retreated into one of her funny moods.

And those funny moods were becoming more and more frequent.

They weren't HA HA funny. They were peculiar. Dan would be her usual effervescent (ten points on the Vocab Test) self and then, suddenly, swifter than the speed of thought, her face would sink and her eyes would thicken with pain and disappointment.

TCR 00:13:39:11

Here's how I discovered what was upsetting Dan so much:

We were sitting on the bus, going into town to see Gerard Way live at The Tunnel, when she suddenly shifted her position on the chair and faced me. She obviously had something important to say, but the words didn't come easily. She'd changed in the last few weeks, going from her happy self to someone who cried constantly. What could I do? The only quote in *The Iconic Black Book of Sorak The Almighty* (Vol. 2) that related to Dan's predicament wasn't appropriate at all:

Tears make a woman's face unattractive and unappealing for men, so cry in private.

Were the teachings of Sorak The Almighty a complete waste of time?

"I'm sorry," Dan sobbed as the world whizzed by, "I can't help it."

"What's wrong?" I asked in the sort of kindly concern of a devoted friend.

"Do you have any deep dark secrets?"

My secrets are buried deep in dark places, crammed between tight spaces. They're so deep I can't find them, so dark I can't see them. Those secrets aren't for Dan or anyone else – just you.

TCR 00:14:08:14

"Why do you want to know if I have any deep dark secrets?" I asked.

"Because I need blackmail material so I can tell you my secret," she said.

I raised my eyebrow and pulled a face. Dan, bless, immediately looked guilty.

"Sorry, I forgot your entire life was splashed on the front pages."

I'm a celebrity. Okay, so I'm not a model or a singer – heck, I don't even have a YouTube channel, and everyone has one of those these days – but I'm famous for *one* thing at least, even if it is surviving a mass poisoning.

It didn't take long for Dan to finally make a decision:

"Okay, I have…something…to tell you."

The bus halted at a station, upon which Dan went quiet, because she wanted to talk while the engine made noise. Whatever she had to tell me, it had to be now. Right now, but not when everyone could hear us.

"I've been keeping this bottled up for so long," Dan sniffled.

Then she blurted out the words that finally set her free.

"I'm gay."

We sat still for a few seconds until I broke the silent stand-off.

"But you don't look happy," I said, nodding and smiling.

Dan's laughter drowned out everything around us, including the loud noise of the grinding bus engine. Then she was crying again, but it was a different sort of crying – she no longer seemed unhappy. She seemed deliriously joyful, finding some sort of humour in the words that had just passed my lips.

Can you blame me for not understanding what she meant at first?

Blame dumb Deacon Glowglass for filling our brains with fire, brimstone, and bullshit.

21

The Gerard Way Fan Club

Dan emerged from inside herself that night. The transformation came complete with heat: now that she'd sparked into existence, fully-formed and wonderful, she seemed to radiate a glow that nobody could see but everyone could feel. Isn't it remarkable how a few whispered words in a friend's ear can realign the axial tilt and put everything into its perfect place? Her funny mood had disappeared from view, replaced by happiness.

More than that, she was *excited*.

Part of that excitement came in the form of a man with red hair and a blue suit.

We had journeyed into town together to go and see Gerard Way live at The Tunnel. It was my first live gig ever and Dan – an old hand at that sort of thing – assured me that I'd enjoy the experience. She also warned me that most of Morvern High would be in attendance. The Tunnel was the hippest place in town, because it was the *only* place that hadn't been closed down by the drug squad. As a result, we'd be sharing a venue with people who wouldn't even look at us in the school corridors.

"I hope he plays *Action Cat*," Dan said over and over again, with the intensity of any prayer you and I have uttered to Sorak The Almighty.

Dan really loved Gerard Way. Her locker at school was covered in posters of his sullen, slightly quizzical face. His transformer hair marked out different eras of his career, all of which Dan helpfully explained to me. But I was freaked out by the loud music and the heaving crowd, some of whom touched me as they passed by towards the bar.

My bladder was heavy from drinking too many cans of Coca-Cola. But I didn't want to go to the toilet. What if I couldn't find Dan again? I'd be lost. Literally. And you would have discovered I'd lied about staying at Dan's house to study for my Vocab Test. Yes. I was at The Tunnel that night. Dan was my trail of breadcrumbs back to you and the house.

When Gerard Way finally took to the stage, it was the most amazing moment of my life.

He conquered the stage in a blue suit, red tie and bright hair.

Dan and the audience obliterated the start of his music with frenzied fan screams.

The sound of screaming had a slightly different effect on me:

TCR 00:15:39:01

I suddenly shot backwards in time, fast enough to feel some kind of whiplash, all the way back to The Day Of Our Final Prayer, the morning that breakfast made us orphans.

The screams brought back to the surface some memories I'd tried to bury.

I don't want to talk about it right now.

We'll get to that though. Eventually.

The gig itself was amazing. Nobody really paid attention to me as I retreated back into my memories. The flashback didn't actually last long. Soon, I found myself swept up in the music, which was loud enough to anchor me back to reality.

We ended the night on a good moment, a memory to cherish:

Gerard smiled at me (right at me!) as he paraded across the stage.

His face would soon be inside my locker door at school.

And Dan?

She got her wish.

Gerard performed *Action Cat* while Dan danced in the dark.

22

Hurricane Rhona

Dan kept her secret at school, but she assured me that it wouldn't be forever. She knew who she was now – and that was all that mattered. I accepted her completely, of course. But something troubled me: I couldn't understand why Dan wanted to keep her sexuality a secret. Why couldn't she be honest and let her classmates know that she was gay. None of them kept their heterosexuality hidden. Far from it!

What would she gain from hiding her real self from everybody?

Then I met Rhona Morton.

And it all made sense.

A lifetime spend under the heel of a religious cult should have taught me that diversity wasn't always something that was celebrated. My first day at Morvern High had reinforced that feeling. And yet it still didn't occur to me that Dan was scared of the reaction she'd get from people if they knew the truth. In my defence, I hadn't quite worked out the high school hierarchy, that constant tug of war between all the cliques under the same roof.

Not everybody values the qualities that make us unique.

Some people at school even sought to stamp out the unalike.

Rhona Morton was the worst. In some respects, Rhona reminded me of Father; both of them hated anything that didn't fit into their narrowly defined viewpoints. Dan assured me that every school in the entire world has a Rhona Morton – mutton dressed as glam and don't we just hate her, though we'd never say that to her face.

Rhona and her clones are never ever alone. They travel in packs in their search for something to keep them amused. They smell weakness and won't hesitate to turn on each other if they are in the right mood. Or should that be wrong mood?

It was during the worst lesson in the entire syllabus – PE obviously – that I had my first encounter with Rhona Morton. It was the start of the lesson, so I'd retreated to the toilet cubicle to change into my shorts and T-shirt in private, as per my religious beliefs. After all, doesn't Sorak The Almighty state in Volume Three of *The Iconic Black Books*:

Paranoia is nature's way of telling you to hide.

Not that I felt paranoid, as such, but the atmosphere in the changing room wasn't optimistic or loud, the way it seemed to be any other time. It felt dark, like the onset of a gathering storm. Hurricane Rhona was on her way and all we could do was take cover.

But it wasn't me that Rhona intended to smack aside.

It was Dan, of course.

Rhona entered the changing room loudly. Her voice broke through the wall into the toilet cubicle where I'd finished hitching up my shorts. My first thought was: *Oh no! Not her. Please don't come in here!* My second was: *Surely Dan will be safe without me?*

"Hello, ladies," Rhona's obnoxious voice brayed, a demented donkey on the loose.

If anyone responded, I didn't hear it. The sound of water passing through rusted pipes wasn't enough to obliterate the sound of Rhona's uniquely obnoxious voice. Sadly. She was still out there while I was in the cubicle, sitting and waiting for everybody to head out to the pitch. But time was agonisingly slow. Had Sorak placed a curse on me?

"Hey," Rhona jeered, "that's my seat."

I frowned. Who had earned Rhona's wrath this time?

"Dyke," she shouted, "get out of my space."

My lungs went tight with fright.

Dan.

It had to be Dan she was picking on.

"Look at that haircut," Rhona continued. "Only dykes have their hair that short."

Dan said nothing. She knew better than to upset Rhona Morton.

"Spikey Dykey!" Rhona jeered, inviting the other girls to laugh.

They duly obliged.

Why didn't anyone stand up to that girl?

Why didn't *I* stand up to her?

Time passed idly, with me stuck in the locked toilet, waiting for everyone to leave. Eventually there was a soft knocking at the door, which I reluctantly opened to reveal the familiar if slightly downtrodden face of my best friend Dan.

"It took me ages to tie my laces," I lied.

"Did you hear what Rhona said to me?" Dan frowned.

"No," I told her, "I didn't hear a thing."

TCR 00:17:00:01

23

Barbie Is An Airhead

The first visitor Father warned us about in his videotaped message arrived in town two days after Dan told me her secret. That's how I remember the date so well. We met at the school gates before I brought her to you. The bell had released us from another day of learning and I saw her there…in the distance… loitering. She resembled one of those *femme fatales* from Father's collection of Hollywood movies. We recognised each other, even from a distance. When you don't belong, and everything reminds you of that fact, you learn to identify people on the periphery of the world. Weirdoes always find their people.

My eyes examined the visitor by the gates with forensic precision.

Evidently, she liked the colour pink. Her floppy brimmed hat, jacket with stiff shoulder-pads, sparkly clutch bag and skirt were all pink. Even her lips were coated with a sugary layer of slick pink. Despite the cloying choice of colour, the pink lady exuded the same oily arrogance as dear departed Father. She insolently glared at passers-by, looking down on them from atop her pink eight-inch heels. They were literally beneath her.

She was beautiful and ugly, close but distant.

What did she want with me?

And could I trust her?

TCR 00:17:21:42

Do you remember the doll you got me for my tenth birthday? I don't know how you got it, where it came from, or what you had to do to find it. I never ever asked. You waited until everyone had gone to bed and you came into The Sanctum with a little cloth bundle. You told me you couldn't find nice paper for the present, so you improvised with a tatty dish towel. You told me to hide the doll after I played with her, because Father would discover you'd been speaking with people outside the four walls. He could never know you had contact with the outside world. It was a crime punishable by exile and I never ever wanted you to leave me.

TCR 00:17:59:08

The birthday doll was slim and oddly proportioned, with a waist that looked unnaturally thin. You told me her name was Barbie. "Barbie?" I sighed in relief. Finally, I'd discovered a name worse than Starrsha. Barbie's hair was white until I used Father's felt pens to dye it brown, carefully colouring each strand. Later, I realised I'd given her the same hair colour as Miss Gibson, my tutor. Barbie didn't mind me colouring her hair. She smiled no matter what happened. Do you know that Barbie is an airhead? There's literally nothing between her ears. If you squeeze her head with your thumb and forefinger, you can feel the space inside the hollow rubber.

Barbie is beautiful, happy and brainless.

TCR 00:18:54:32

Maybe that's what put my nerves on edge the day I saw the stranger at the school gates.

Because she reminded me of my birthday doll except…

She stopped smiling when she saw me.

24

Imelda Glowglass

Her large pink sunglasses masked her eyes, but I knew she was looking right at me. The lads in the schoolyard didn't even attempt to disguise their fascination with the woman at the gate. Their whispers and gestures made it clear they liked her in *that* way. Sorak wouldn't approve of their base desires, but I watched their behaviour with fascination: the volume on their voices turned up, an attempt to draw her attention. They whistled at the woman, taking in her curves inch by inch, laughing and whispering, jabbing each other with elbows as they shared stories about what they'd like to do to her in private.

Far from being offended, the stranger at the gate seemed to enjoy it.

Sorak has a quote in Volume One of his *Iconic Black Books* that the lads wouldn't appreciate, but here it is anyway:

Lust is a hideous trick to tempt people away from the path of righteousness.

But I prefer this one:

Abstinence is an invitation to a greater understanding of Sorak. Please R.S.V.P. immediately.

Sadly, the loudmouthed lads weren't the only ones under the stranger's spell.

"Who is *that?*" Dan gasped.

"Oh no," I remarked, slightly disappointed to see my friend drooling over the stranger. But what Dan said next was even more startling. It actually made me gasp aloud.

She said: "What a doll!"

Was that just an expression she used? It *had* to be, because Dan couldn't read minds. She had no idea I'd mentally connected the stranger to a doll I once got for my birthday.

"I've never seen that woman before in my entire life," I said quietly.

I wasn't lying. I hadn't actually met this person at the gate, not in person. But certain nasty suspicions were forming in my brain, gelling together into one theory. I had a good idea who was standing a few metres from me. If my suspicions were correct, then Father had sent his worst enemy to plague us both.

The woman smiled a cotton candy grin again as I moved closer to her.

Out of everyone in Morvern High, she saw me and knew the truth.

"Hello," the woman said breathily, "I'm Imelda Glowglass. You must be Starrsha."

I gave her no indication that I recognised her. That would have felt like giving her – and by extension *him* – a petty little victory. Nonetheless, she tried again:

"You have your mother's face," Imelda said, not unkindly.

"I don't know her," I said coldly.

"Ah, but you have your Father's pointed tone of voice."

TCR 00:20:18:41

My classmates and all the other students leaving Morvern High suddenly seemed to notice me again. It wasn't a good feeling, the sensation of being scrutinised. The person facing me...Aunt Imelda...had star power in abundance, as potent as any of the women from Hollywood that her brother had idolised before he ate his breakfast for the last time. The full force of the strange power she exuded nearly overwhelmed me, but I fought back hard. No-one would ever trick me again with a smile or a friendly gesture.

"Yes," I muttered. "I'm Starrsha."

Then I asked an obvious question:

"Why are you here?"

Imelda took a deep breath before describing the events that had brought her to me.

"That daft old fool sent a videotape begging me to come back home. How quaint is that? A videotape. It took me a full week to track down an old video cassette player. A friend in town had one in his attic. He dragged it down so I could use it."

45

Dan was dumbstruck at the sight of Aunt Imelda, along with everyone else. It was disgusting. Normally, I'd quote something from *The Iconic Black Books* – but Dan probably wouldn't care anyway. Who does, quite frankly?

"The Deacon told me I'd find you here," Imelda continued.

"Here?" I cried out. "But I didn't enrol at Morvern High until after Father died!"

"He said specifically that you'd be at school and you'd take me back to The Sanctum. He insisted I come and wait for you at the gate."

TCR 00:21:05:22

How did he know?

Maybe he could see the future?

No, that's stupid.

TCR 00:21:08:05

"He said you'd be easy to spot, because you're the girl with no friends."

"He said *what?*"

He was making fun of me from beyond the grave.

"I'm your friend," Dan offered helpfully.

Imelda smiled, but it never reached her eyes.

"Now you must escort me back home so we can talk about important things."

"It isn't *your* home," I told her, but she ignored my words.

"Can I come with you?" Dan asked with a slightly hopeful tone of voice.

"No," Imelda said, breaking poor Dan's heart for the first time. "But I'm sure you'll be able to visit at some point soon. We have Family business to discuss."

I'm sure she emphasised the *F* in Family.

TCR 00:21:59:16

Imelda – someone I'd heard so much about – had been gone for fifteen years.

She'd left the day after Father put her on trial for witchcraft.

25

Crime And Punishment

The only time I ever heard Imelda mentioned by name was when Father was drunk. He was often very drunk. He said her name in the same way he swore whenever he stood on cow dung in the field. 'Aunt Imelda' was a phantom, a lesson to be learned whenever someone ignored the commandments of Sorak The Almighty.

Imelda, it was said, possessed mystical powers that were unholy in the eyes of Sorak.

I suspect her only power was to get old wealthy men to fall in love with her.

TCR 00:22:05:22

Here's a true story. Years ago, late one night, a funny thing happened. Father ordered me to peel the potatoes for dinner, so I headed downstairs to the pantry and dragged an enormous sack of spuds upstairs to the kitchen. But it was the hottest day of the year. Honestly, the oats were golden and the crop thick, but we were all gasping for air. After reaching the kitchen with that sack of spuds, I bathed my hands and face in cold water. The tap by the sink spat water out in spurts and the pipes rattled a bit too loudly, but the water was nice and refreshing on my skin. It took ten minutes of heavy graft, and a sprained wrist, to get that sack next to the pot where the potatoes were boiled for dinner.

I took a knife in my hand without complaint and started peeling the potatoes.

Not once did I moan, because it would only backfire on me, like asking for sugar on our morning oatmeal.

Father kept a close eye as I peeled. He sat behind me with the sound of his breathing an oppressive reminder of his presence. Then, without warning, he suddenly started ranting about "that evil witch" and "her treacherous ways".

I didn't know much about Aunt Imelda, but she sounded like a hoot to me!

"There's a special place in hell for those who defy the glory of Sorak," his voice hissed from the kitchen table. Then he stood up and crossed the length of the kitchen in a few steps. He was close. Very close. I felt his breath on my neck and the pitter-patter of spittle in my left ear. I ignored him, instead pretending that the peeling of potatoes was an incredibly interesting task when in fact my fingers were breaking.

My lack of reaction seemed to rile him into a fully-fledged screaming fit.

"That woman," Father continued, "was never a True Believer. How could she be when she craved far more than what Sorak was willing to bestow? She's now living a filthy life full of men and alcohol. Filthy, dirty, evil!"

Yes, a drunken man with three wives accusing his sister of being filthy, dirty and evil.

He kept ranting until my ears went numb as a result of his endless tirades.

Eventually I had to interrupt him:

"How many potatoes do you want peeled?" I asked warily.

"All of them," Father said after a few moments of deliberation.

"All of them!"

"All of them," he repeated. "That way you'll learn to listen to what I have to say."

The sack I'd dragged up from the basement contained over one hundred potatoes.

I was eight years old.

26

Simon Says

"How dreadfully bourgeois!" Imelda declared when she stepped into The Sanctum for the first time in over a decade. "I'm already starting to remember why I wanted away from this dump. Why can't you update the décor? Haven't you heard of IKEA?"

"What's IKEA?" I asked.

Our house hadn't been redecorated in over ten years, and was completely untouched since the day our family died. Obviously we cleaned it and kept everything in good condition, but we hadn't ever refurbished our home. For Aunt Imelda, it must have been like stepping through a gateway into her past. And you're part of that past.

You came down the staircase with a startled expression.

Your fingers wriggled and spelled out a name letter by letter.

IMELDA! I DIDN'T THINK YOU'D COME BACK.

"Hello, Simon," she said with a polite nod, "you haven't changed much."

My heart felt heavy with hurt as it suddenly dawned on me that you had a shared history together; a connection that predated our bond. Isn't that silly? To be jealous of your own aunt? But you're all I've got and we're the last two alive. Or I thought we were.

I'VE CHANGED, you said with fingers. YOU HAVE NO IDEA HOW MUCH I'VE CHANGED. BUT IT'S GOOD TO SEE YOU AGAIN, IMELDA.

At least *someone* was pleased to see Auntie dearest.

27

Honesty Is The Worst Policy

There's something odd about my classmates, something I've noticed in the short time I've been at Morvern High. Every time they're about to say something really nasty, they start off with the words, "I hope you don't take this personally but…"

It's like an apology before a slap in the face, isn't it? Or a drive-by shooting preceded with a bunch of flowers or a basket of fruit.

And it never helps. That's what makes what I've got to do next even worse.

Guess what?

I hope you don't take this personally but…

You've always tried your best with me since everybody whispered their last prayers, but now that I'm finally being completely honest with you, I have something to say.

Okay. Are you ready?

Your cooking is terrible.

Honestly, it's **so** bad.

I can't count the amount of times I've pretended to eat what you've put down on my plate, chewing and chewing until you look away and I'm able to spit the pulped remains into the nearest bin.

Why do you think I learned to cook?

You're the best brother in the world and the worst chef.

Everyone has a talent in life. My talent is cookery. I love it. Nothing is too complicated for me. When I cook, it's chaos and creation in the kitchen. Mama taught me how to take lots of different things and turn them into something almost artistic. The kitchen is my favourite place in the world, the only place I feel like me, whoever that is these days.

I'm a sorceress in the kitchen and Mama's old copy of *Delia Smith's Complete Cookery Course* is my trusty tome of spells. I never really got to cook while Father was alive, because he thought anything that wasn't boiled eggs and toast was too French.

I've cooked more meals in the last few months than I ever did while Father was alive.

Remember the first night I brought Imelda back home with me? I begged you to let me make our supper. You eventually agreed, thinking it was my attempt at impressing my glamourous auntie. That isn't true though.

There was an ulterior motive.

I wanted to scare her into leaving us alone.

28

Bon Appetit!

"You've grown *so* much," Imelda cooed in my ear, "especially in the belly area."
What a cow! But I ignored her as she whispered passive-aggressive insults at
me. Instead, I focused on my task: laying the table for supper. I'd laid tables
since I was four years old. It was something that I came to enjoy, the routine
and precision of placing everything in order. *This*, I used to think, *is how Sorak
felt when He created the world*. The three large tables in the main hall took more
work than the small table in The Sanctum where we ate our dinner, the place
Father used to take his private meals away from the congregation.

I hadn't set foot in the main hall since the morning I watched everyone go
to Heaven.

"It's such a novelty being in the house," Imelda said cheerily, "it's much
nicer than the dorm rooms. I had no idea the house was so plush. The old fool
never let me stay here."

Imelda switched her gaze until it swept over me.

"But then you've always stayed here, haven't you?"

"Yes," I mumbled. What else could I say? It was the truth.

"We all had to sleep rough in that cold dorm room while you had a nice
bed and room."

"Sleeping on a hard floor will result in free accommodation in Sorak's
House when you cross into the afterlife," I quoted ponderously from – what else
– *The Iconic Black Books of Sorak The Almighty*. The words sounded as ridiculous
that day as they do now, but she had me cornered with a justifiable fact. Even
though Father never let me cook for anyone, he *did* ensure that I had some
luxuries in comparison to the others.

"All I could smell was the doughy stink of oatmeal," Imelda snapped, "every
single day in my hair and on my skin. The Deacon didn't run a church. He ran
a sweatshop – though he never once broke a sweat. Why did we put up with it?"

"You used to live here, didn't you?" It wasn't a rude question, because outside of a few hazy memories, I couldn't remember much about my aunt. Imelda had become something of an urban legend for me and the younger members of the congregation.

"Yes," she said with a frown, "working every day until I was too exhausted to do anything else. Working while he sat on his fat ass watching his crappy old videotapes. All those old black and white movies! He could afford anything and he still watched videotapes."

The pitch of Imelda's voice climbed until it reached an almost operatic zenith.

"What made *you* so special that you got to stay in here with all this luxury while the rest of us were locked outside in a room without a view?"

I blotted out her words and focussed on positioning the cutlery on the table.

Dinner was nearly ready.

"I'm his real family and I've come home to claim what's mine by right of birth."

The last fork was placed tenderly on the table beside Imelda, though I had a fantasy of thrusting it into her neck, if only to shut her up once and for all.

"We're nearly ready," I announced in a small voice.

The bowls had been carefully laid down in their ideal positions.

It would be a special meal no-one would forget.

YOU'VE BEEN WORKING ON THIS FOR HOURS you said, wide-eyed with anticipation for what was bubbling in the pot. Did you think it was soup or broth? If you thought either of those things, then my surprise was a complete success. Halleluiah!

I didn't really notice your face at first. I was too busy checking for Imelda's reaction.

The ladle went into the pot. Then I doled out the first helping.

"I can't wait to eat," Imelda said as she licked her red lips, "I'm starving!"

That's when she realised what I'd put into her bowl.

A steaming hot pile of oatmeal.

You jumped backwards out of your chair, knocking it over.

I couldn't see you, but I imagine you were shocked or hurt by what I did that night.

The muffled sound of a gasp – perhaps horror or disgust – came from your lips. And yet you must have known from the aroma what I was concocting.

Perhaps Imelda realised too. If she did, she wasn't fazed by my stunt.

Instead she slowly, deliberately, placed her spoon deep into the bowl…and ate a large helping of the delicious dinner I'd made especially for her.

"Yum," she said defiantly, gently lapping each drop from the spoon.

Her eyes, however, said:

Foolish little girl, I'm not scared of you.

29

Destroy All Invaders

Okay.

It wasn't the best plan of attack, but I was desperate to get rid of that woman. She'd been brought back into our lives by Father. Anything he had planned for us was bound to end in misery and suffering. But you know that now, don't you? I wish you'd listened to me.

"We need to get her out of our house," I said that night in the kitchen, as I washed the dishes. The thick doughy porridge had already hardened into crusts, which had to be scrubbed firmly. You didn't reply, seemingly too deep in thought to respond.

I tried again.

"She's an invader," I whined.

SHE'S FAMILY, you said with fingers.

"Our Family died in the middle of a prayer," I hissed.

The expression on your face hinted at some inner turmoil.

We both know why that is, don't we?

TCR 00:30:09:43

30

Being Boring

I used to think all I needed to stand out at school was a cool pair of sunglasses, or expensive designer shoes. It's a puzzle to be solved: Find the right combination of accessories and...*BAM*...everybody would love me. Heck, I'd settle for being liked by them, or even tolerated. Every now and again I'd try and speak to someone, only for them to move quietly away.

People see me, but they don't really *see* me.

Maybe that's why Dan asked me to deliver her letter to Aimee Curtis.

But this was no normal letter, not like the sort you send in the post.

It was so secret that I wasn't allowed to read it.

31

Tribespotting

Everybody at school considered Aimee Curtis to be the Princess Di of Morvern High. She was graceful and chic, with a wardrobe that doubled as Morvern's Vivienne Westwood outlet. It didn't take long for Aimee to become our version of royalty. By *our* I mean *everyone at Morvern High*. Aimee seemed to be a genuinely lovely girl. She was nice to me when everybody else laughed at my clothes and hair. Not that she ever came to my defence, but I noticed when she didn't join in with their laughter.

That one gesture was all I had during my hellish first few days.

TCR 00:32:25:16

Navigating the social trajectory of Morvern High was a challenge, especially with my background. But I had a perfect chaperon in Dan. She explained *everything* to me one day in the lunch hall, whilst we ate burgers and fries (not *chips*; they're called *fries* for some reason) and soon enough I became clued up on every social tribe at school.

This stuff is equally as important as any Vocab Test. For the sake of my story, you need to know those tribes too. Or you can just press >> Fast Forward and bypass this bit.

Ready? Good. Here we go!

The Clique are the cheerleaders, WAGS, beauty queens, and pretty girls. Mostly boring, they've never had to work for anything in their lives, preferring to let their faces do the hard work; and one day they'll have lots of hard work done on those faces. When beauty is your currency, the worst thing you can be is poor. They're the future models and trophy wives to footballers. Either that or they'll end up on reality TV. We shouldn't hate them because they're beautiful – let us instead hate them for being HORRIBLE HUMAN BEINGS. If any of them paid a ghost writer to write a biography of their life, it would be titled *My Struggle...Without Lip Gloss.*

Rhona Morton is a high-ranking member of The Clique, which would be a bonus reason to despise them. Yet Aimee is a high-ranking member too, and everyone at school loves her. Perhaps I'm not doing them any justice?

Then we have **The Sportos**. They're the jocks and athletes of the school. They're untouchable on the football pitch and everywhere else in life. They're mostly okay if a little noisy. Their natural allies are, of course, **The Clique,** whom they date for their reaffirming conversation and rich intellectual capabilities. As you can hear from my tone, my time at Morvern High taught me how to be slightly bitchy. In this area, I score an A+, which isn't necessarily a good thing.

The Boy Racers, also known as The Motorheads and The Speed Freaks, love their cars more than they love their parents. They enjoy nothing better than zooming down school corridors on jet-powered skateboards. Hobbies include looking at cars online and seething about Jeremy Clarkson's 'unfair' dismissal from the BBC.

Get over it, ladz. It happened years ago.

Avoid The Boy Racers or be hit at eighty miles per hour.

The Vegang are an odd group in a school crammed with unusual social gangs. What happens when all the militant vegans at Morvern High School get together to form a gang? They become a **Vegang**. Don't mess with them! And for the love of Sorak, don't wear anything made of leather in their presence. I once witnessed a group of girls from The Vegang cutting up Johnny Sharp's red leather jacket with a pair of scissors. Johnny, the quiff-wearing retro-rock-'n'-rolling Elvis wannabe from third year, retaliated by eating ten bacon sandwiches in front of them. He'll end up looking like Elvis if that continues.

The Brotherhood of Warcraft is a group of boys with an obsession for really violent videogames. They refuse to allow girls to join their group, which isn't fair because girls like games too. However, in a shocking turn of events, one angry fourth-year pupil named Lydia Moore actually started **The Sisterhood of Warcraft** in protest at the chauvinism. But it all went horribly wrong for one faction when The Brotherhood declared war on The Sisterhood. Result? The Sisterhood won the >> *FAST FORWARD* >>

<PLAY> Then there's me, Starrsha Glowglass, survivor of a mass suicide. I'm The Oatmeal Girl, which means I don't belong to any group or clique. I'm outside and no-one will hand me a set of keys. But at least I had Dan.

She's the only person who understood me.

And that's why I agreed to deliver her secret letter to Aimee.

We were huddled in the corner of the gymnasium at the start of another PE lesson, talking about the secret letter. It was all we'd talked about for two weeks. Dan was especially nervous, because Aimee was at the other end of the room, swinging on a rope while her friends laughed obnoxiously loudly.

"Promise me you won't look at the note," Dan begged.

She was my best friend, but she wasn't really like me at all. She loved PE because she was a sporty girl who could kick a ball, run fast, back flip, and win at everything. Then there's me. A girl trapped between two worlds, neither of which wants to give me oxygen. Tall, thin, gawky and lacking in the social skills required to survive at high school. Worse, I have limp hair, and a face that repels all brands of make-up. Max Factor would tell me I lacked 'The X-Factor'. Maybelline would probably suggest I'm not worth it.

Nothing worked for me.

But the letter Dan wanted me to deliver…

It meant she needed me. And that meant everything.

"I'll take it to her right now," I offered, "she's over there with her friends."

Dan nearly pulled my arm from its socket in panic.

"Are you nuts? No, you have to take it to her when no-one is watching."

I waited and waited and waited.

Once I'd become bored of waiting, I waited some more.

It soon became apparent that Aimee Curtis was *never* alone.

But I wouldn't be thwarted. I had promised my best friend that I would deliver her mystery letter. Not even Sorak had a quote that best described my steely determination.

32

Bad Perfume Blues

After I served up bowls of oatmeal for dinner, you suddenly decided that it wouldn't be right for me to make supper for the three of us anymore. Totally understandable! It didn't bother me that much. I'd made my statement and didn't fancy cooking lovely meals for my witch of an aunt. Besides, it gave me time to stay in my room and plot how I could reach Aimee without being seen by her friends.

The note was small and folded, neatly sealed inside a purple envelope.

What did it say? Why was it such a secret?

I was thinking about Dan when a fruity scent surged up my nostrils. My eyes burned. It wasn't from the envelope. No, only one person doused themself with that amount of Prada Candy, and she'd entered my bedroom while I'd been lost in a daydream.

TCR 00:43:25:56

"Hey, Starrsha," Imelda waved. "What are you doing up here all by yourself?"

"Go away," I grumbled. What would it take to rid us of this pest?

She was an insect, a bug to be crushed, ground slowly under heel. Oh, I'd gladly do it.

"You don't really want me to leave though," Imelda said in a very reasonable tone of voice. "And even if you do want me to leave, it doesn't matter. My brother insisted that I come here and fulfil his last wish."

"We still don't know what he said to you!"

"And you never will, child. That's part of his final request."

"Liar!" I spat. "You're up to something – and I'll find out what!"

She was dressed in her trademark pink, the same shade used to paint Barbie's Dream Car; it pleased the eyes on first inspection, but quickly clouded the eyeballs. Too bright, it was the colour of an attention-seeker. Imelda's eyes weren't pink, but instead sparkled keenly with glittering green, always alert, forever hunting.

Her eyes set off the green pendant she had affixed to a silver blouse.

TCR 00:44:14:28

It would be extremely petty to deny the simple truth about my Auntie Imelda: she never looked anything other than flawless, regardless of her cheap tastes.

Obviously, I'd never say that to her face. I'm very anti Auntie.

What more could I do to chase this woman away from my room and out of my life?

"Father is dead. Our Family is dead. Why can't you just leave us alone?"

But Imelda wasn't interested in what I had to say. That wasn't the reason she had intruded into my room. No, she had something else in mind. And I knew what that was when I realised her lovely green eyes weren't looking at me anymore.

They were looking at the envelope in my hands.

"A note?" she said with a smirk. "Are you writing love letters to boys?"

"NO!" I gasped. How could she think that of me? The sense of violation I felt was all-consuming, just as she'd intended. Imelda had picked up a few of Father's tricks, it seemed. And I gave her the reaction she wanted.

Something in me stirred into rage and that rage surged into movement.

Imelda laughed as I leapt off my bed and pushed at her.

"GET OUT!" I screamed. "GET OUT AND GO AWAY!"

"Little Star," Imelda sung as she descended the stairs down to the kitchen, "Father's favourite little star!"

Then, because her other jibe wasn't painful enough, she added mockingly:
"Blessed be the Children of Sorak, even the ones scattered on the wind!"

Then I was all alone. Exactly what I wanted.

33

Dead Insects

Insects have fascinated me ever since I was a little girl. The first bug that made a lasting impression on me was a mealworm I found in a bag of rotten old milo maize. The youngest members of the Church were often sent into the field to pick weevils, worms and bugs off the oats before the crop was washed and purified. The importance of this bug-picking ritual was stressed by Father many times during his morning service: "If any of them get into the sacks, we'll be sued and lose our Church. And if we lose our Church, we'll lose our connection to Sorak The Almighty."

What he failed to tell us was that if he lost the Church, he would also lose his free workforce.

But none of that crossed my blissful child brain as I held my prize with pride:

The mealworm squirmed in a desperate bid to get into the oats and out of the light.

I put it into darkness forever when I applied a little pressure from my forefinger and thumb: the worm burst into a wet pulpy mess. My feelings of guilt were so overwhelming that I prayed to Sorak for forgiveness. But it was too late for me. The splattered remains of the mealworm had already stained my nails and probably my soul.

Mama Sadie, my favourite of Father's three wives, hated insects.

I suppose that's why she kept that massive bottle of insecticide in the house.

TCR 00:47:08:48

We won't talk about *that* right now. You know as well as I do how important that bottle is later in my story. Oh yes, we'll get there soon enough. In the meantime, I want to continue my little anecdote about insects.

Not only did Aunt Imelda remind me of a doll you once bought me, but her honey-coloured hair also put me in mind of buzzy bumble bees. I hate bees. They sting. There was something predacious about the newest arrival at our old house. That's another word I learned at school during the class Vocab Test, and I'm going to use the hell out of them: *Predacious* means predatory. And if Auntie's hair was the colour of honey, then her actual personality puts me in mind of a different insect: the black widow spider, obviously. Come on! Imelda is the sort of woman who would kill her husband to inherit his fortune, then use her new-found wealth to ensnare a rich old man to start the cycle all over again.

Don't you agree?

If I could choose to be any insect, then I'd want to be a beautiful butterfly and flutter by.

But even my daydreams have their borders – limits that my imagination can't cross.

After all, can a beautiful butterfly truly be related to a black widow spider?

34

Trick Question

The following day was eventful for all the wrong reasons.

Dan met me during our first break as I stood by the Irn-Bru vending machine, my bag sitting on the floor as I wrestled with spare change. She was dressed in a familiar black velour tracksuit with her name on it, complete with large sporty backpack slung around her left shoulder. Nervously, or expectantly, she took me aside and spoke with a voice brimming with urgency.

"Did you deliver the letter?"

"Not yet," I said, "but I promise I'll do it today."

Dan didn't look happy, but she couldn't say anything because she was relying on me to be a good friend and help her out. The longer I carried the secret letter, the more it weighed me down. Honestly, I could feel it tugging at me. The worst fear in the world I have is disappointing the people who matter most. You're important to me, Simon, obviously. But Dan mattered too and the thought of failing her made my heart heavy.

What happened next should help you understand why I was so distraught when everything went wrong. I failed as a friend. And that's not something that's easy to admit.

TCR 00:48:31:25

I finally found Aimee by herself – Praise Sorak – in the school library during a study break. The library was where I stocked up on *Sweet Valley High* books. **I love *Sweet Valley High* so much.** Anyway, Aimee's friends had decided to head out to the local corner shop (which isn't actually on a corner, incidentally) to try and get an adult to buy them a packet of cigarettes.

Their gross habits aside, their absence was a rare spot of good luck for me.

The school library was a small stuffy room with sealed windows and grimy old books, the result of an institution without enough money to replenish the shelves with new stock. The green carpet was threadbare and soiled from thousands of feet passing through on their way to the PCs. The computers were in an adjoining room next door and served as the unofficial headquarters for The Brotherhood of Warcraft.

"Hello," I said politely as Aimee scribbled some notes.

She looked up at me and though surprised, still greeted me with a warm grin.

"Hello, Starrsha," she purred.

TCR 00:49:31:43

Yes, it was a proper purrrrrrrrrr and I found myself joyful that I'd been acknowledged by Morvern High royalty. She even rolled the *rrrrrrrrs* in my name until it popped off her tongue. It was the only time in my life that I liked the sound of it.

TCR 00:50:50:11

"Do you mind if I sit for a few seconds?" I asked, trying to keep it together.

"Of course. Please sit."

Aimee's eyes weren't on me even though I'd taken a seat in front of her. I followed her gaze up to the upper wall behind me. There was a poster on it that I'd never noticed before.

It was A3-sized and blank except for some large black letters in Arial Black font.

The poster read:

A Woman's Place
Is At
_O_ _

"That's easy," I said, "the answer is HOME."

"I thought that too," Aimee sighed, "but according to Dan, the answer is WORK."

TCR 00:51:29:35

Already we were struggling to make a connection. Without a hint of a lie, my face burned brighter than any star that has earned me my nickname. Why did I need to be friends with Aimee? Why couldn't I just give her the letter?

These were the questions I asked myself time and time again.

Why did I have this damn need to be liked at school?

TCR 00:51:50:00

Aimee sat still, her eyes fixed on the poster.

"I have something for you," I said, suddenly remembering my reason for the meeting.

"Really?" She seemed curious despite herself.

Slowly, gradually, I thrust my hand into the depths of my satchel.

My fingers felt around every inch of the interior.

And found nothing.

It took a few seconds for my brain to log the terrible turn of events.

Dan's letter had vanished!

35

Sorak The Almighty's Advice For Dealing With Scumbags

It took hours of frantic searching until I finally realised the truth of my predicament:

I'd lost Dan's letter.

How could I have been so careless? I hunted high, low and everywhere in between. The contents of my locker festooned the dirty floor of the corridor, a metaphor for my life. Not one passer-by paused to walk around the junk; instead they stepped and stamped all over my books and pens. Desperately I resorted to reconstructing my movements across the entire morning. But no matter where I walked, all paths led to confusion. How could I lose something so important? It couldn't simply have dropped out of my satchel.

Then, unexpectedly, a spark in the brain lit up an idea:

What if Auntie Imelda had stolen it? She knew about the letter, of course. It made sense.

"That bitch!" I seethed. "I bet she took it out of sheer spite."

TCR 00:52:21:18

There's a pertinent quote to be found in Volume Two of *The Iconic Black Books of Sorak The Almighty* that best summed up my feelings on that particular day:

If a sinner ever gives you crap, deliver unto their face a mighty slap.

In my mind I saw Imelda's head snapping back and forth in slow motion as I struck her with a divinely-powered smack to her face. Dan had entrusted me with her secret mission and I'd bungled spectacularly. But it wasn't my fault. I was a victim of foul play.

A dark voice in my brain made words appear in my ear:

"If only she'd gobbled up some special oatmeal."

But that wasn't me. It would never be me.

Scaring Imelda was one thing, but actually poisoning her? I couldn't do it.

The mental image of her eating a bowl of poisoned porridge had the unfortunate side effect of shooting me back all the way into the past to the Day Of The Final Prayer, the last place I wanted to visit in my memory. It became a difficult image to shift even as I headed back to The Sanctum. I didn't even stick around at school to meet Dan, because then I'd have to explain why I hadn't delivered her letter to Aimee, despite my promise.

Without looking back, I fled the schoolyard of Morvern High, bursting with speed all the way through town, never stopping or slowing. A massive surge or anger fuelled me to push harder until the houses and streets became woods and trees. Beyond the woods lay the four walls, which prevented trespassers from entering Glowglass Estate…and inhabitants from leaving.

My body and brain were disconnected. I'd never run that fast before, nor have I since. No. That's not true. I ran faster once, just once, but I won't talk about that yet. Anyway, I left the work to my legs and they moved me to the garden until I stood a few inches from Aunt Imelda.

She looked up at me from the ground as my shadow fell upon her body.

"You look like crap," was her brisk assessment.

It occurred to me that the only thing we had in common was the language we spoke, though even that was debateable. We would never ever be close, regardless of our common history as members of The Family. I hated her and she hated me.

TCR 00:53:17:55

She was sunbathing, reading a trashy magazine, with a large floppy-brimmed black hat perched on her head and matching sunglasses on her nose. She wore virtually nothing on her body except a tiny piece of cloth across her breasts and a pair of frayed denim shorts, cut-off well above the knee. It was terribly immodest.

She had a pink cocktail, crammed with large ice-cubes, in a glass beside her right hand.

I scooped it up and hurled its contents across her bare neck and shoulders.

Aunt Imelda howled in shock as she seized up against the shock drop in temperature. Her face burned with resentment; it was the only warm part of her body thanks to my improvised cold-cocktail baptism.

Between us, I enjoyed throwing those contents far too much.

"What the hell are you playing at?" she snarled.

"Where's the letter?"

"What letter?"

"Don't make me ask again or I'll throw something bigger at you."

"I don't know what you're talking about!"

"You stole an envelope out of my school bag and now you're denying it."

"The only thing I'm here to steal is the money my brother has stashed away in this rotten dump."

Her moment of sudden honesty reduced me to shocked silence.

But I quickly found my voice:

"You're going to rob us?"

"No, because that would imply that I'm taking *your* property. And none of this belongs to you. It's mine. I will have it. I *must* have it. And you'll have nothing but a retard brother who can't speak or hear me when I call him names all day. It's so funny, I just wait until he turns around and then I tell him what I really think about you lot."

That's honestly what she said to me.

I wanted to reach out and break her neck. It was thin enough.

"You're in my way," she said.

I think she was referring to me blocking the sun, but I'm not sure.

36

Pray Like Aretha Franklin

The idea of admitting to Dan that I'd lost her letter made me physically sick. The lump in my guts became so bad that I took a few days off school. It seemed like a good idea at the time. But it meant I was stuck in this big house all day and night, with nothing but my manic mind and some *Sweet Valley High* books. When you're alone you start thinking about things; and when you start thinking about things, you start remembering things. And I remembered something strange. At the time I thought nothing of it. But now I was alone in my room for twenty-four hours, holed up in a bid to avoid Aunt Imelda, I had ample time to reconsider. It was something Father said in his videotape message. His words banged off the sides of my skull, causing an echo, trying to make me aware of something that didn't quite...sit...right.

He said: "A few weeks ago I was told by Sorak that I'd die quickly and suddenly."

TCR 00:57:12:17

The police investigation into the deaths concluded it was the result of a mass suicide planned by Father, a final sacrifice to Sorak. Yes? The news bulletins on TV were full of lurid headlines about 'murderous Deacon Glowglass' and gory details about how lethal insecticide found its way into a pot of porridge that we ate every morning before our prayers, the acidic taste masked by salt. Right? Then a journalist even got a photograph of the bodies, our Family strewn across the tables, their faces wet with blood and bile.

One reporter claimed Father was in heavy debt, that the taxman wanted his money.

That all happened. We were there in the midst of it all, gaining fame and notoriety. The perfect victims: you, deaf and mute, handsome and hardworking but cripplingly shy. Then there was me, the adopted daughter of The Deacon. In all of the media we had one thing in common. Not family or Family. It was a word. Just one word.

It bound us together in every headline.

And that word?

SURVIVORS.

We survived a mass-murder suicide because we didn't eat the poisoned porridge.

We didn't eat the porridge because we don't like salt in our food.

Anyway, the investigation was swift and decisive.

Both of us were left alone.

But...

The police never got a chance to see Father's videotaped message to us, the one we watched in his Secret Cinema. Does that really matter? Would it make a difference if they heard the old man speak? If they heard him say he *knew* someone was out to get him?

Do you know what it means?

Maybe...just maybe...he wasn't responsible for all the deaths.

TCR 00:58:02:34

Sleep hasn't been easy for me in the last few months, despite my fluffy pillows and fabulous memory foam mattress. It became especially difficult in the month after the Final Prayer and all the other stuff. I'm getting ready to talk about it. I'm here right now recording this, and everything is going to be true and honest.

I've been here for nearly an hour talking to you. How long will this videotape last? Some videotapes last for hours and hours, but I'm not sure about this one. It could cut out before I get to the end...I'll talk quicker.

TCR 00:59:08:04

Sometimes, when I manage to get a bit of sleep, it makes me feel worse. Sleep isn't an escape for me because my dreams are filled with a whirlwind of faces.

There's Father, obviously, and Aunt Imelda's smug smirk, rendered infinitely more irritating in the spiral. These dreams always crash down on me until I'm back at church, standing in the midst of bodies scattered across tables. My hands cover my mouth to stifle the screams. Then, at the end of my dream, a giant envelope addressed to AIMEE flattens me.

Do you know the ironic thing about this whole mess?

Every day I prayed to Sorak The Almighty. Oh, I prayed and begged and praised and prayed until my clasped hands went numb. I didn't ask for much. Just one thing.

Can you guess what I prayed for?

I prayed for Father's death.

And my prayers were answered!

Sadly, Sorak overreacted and killed everyone else too.

TCR 01:00:00:00

37

Happiness

You started leaving the house early in the morning and returning late at night.

But even in the gloom from the window of my bedroom I saw a smile on your face. There was something different about the way you walked; the lads at my school would say you had a 'swagger', but I would say you had a newly found 'confidence'. You walked with your head held high.

Something had changed.

It took me a few hours to understand what I didn't recognise at first glance.

You were happy.

I wish I could be happy.

38
The Party

Eventually I returned to Morvern High and came clean to Dan about losing her letter. Remarkably, it didn't seem to matter anymore. She drew me close into an embrace and I finally got to feel a little bit happy for the first time since Father died. According to Dan, things had changed in my absence, but she was maddeningly secretive.

TCR 01:02:18:44

My favourite school lesson is History. None of it happened like it did in Volume One of *The Iconic Black Books of Sorak The Almighty*. For instance, millions and millions of years ago the world was populated by large monsters called *dinosaurs* that ate plants and each other. No, honestly, I've been assured that they were real. Huge bones have been found that prove these dinosaurs really did exist. Yet this completely flies in the face of what Sorak said in Chapter Four of Volume One at paragraph eight. Sorak didn't, in fact, patrol the heavens in His Golden Castle Of Greatness, nestled on a cloud in the sky. The poor old dinosaurs were killed by a giant rock from the sky, which might possibly have been hurled down by Sorak. Maybe. But there's no reference to that in his books. Amazingly, humans evolved from apes and not from the spit of Sorak as He explained in Volume One. Now, I don't know about you, but I'd rather come from an ape than some drool. Yuck.

History is full of surprises.

Dan had a surprise too.

TCR 01:02:59:41

"I'm going to a party," she told me on my first day back at school, near the end of our History lesson. Our classmates had already started packing up their belongings in anticipation of the lunch bell. I had a feeling she'd been dying to tell me her secret all day long. However, I hadn't expected her to say anything about a party. In fact, I was still reeling from her lack of reaction to the disappearance of her mysterious envelope she'd entrusted to me. Not only did she not seem to care, she didn't seem to find any fault with me. Thank goodness. We were still best friends. I was her ultimate confidante.

"Who invited you to their party?" I asked.

"Rhona."

I repeated my question, because I thought I'd misheard Dan the first time:

"Rhona," she said, duplicating her first reply.

"But…I don't understand…I mean you hate Rhona."

"Hate is a strong word," Dan said with a slight tut. "Besides, I'm not going alone."

Ah. She was about to ask me, wasn't she? That was my thought too.

"I'm going with Aimee."

A glimpse of hurt must have crossed my face because Dan hastily added:

"I didn't think it would be your sort of thing, Starrsha. Anyway, Aimee asked me. I couldn't say no to her. She could have asked anyone, and she asked me."

"Don't worry about it," I grinned thinly. "I'd do the same."

But that isn't true. I would have asked her to come with me. I'm her best friend and I suddenly felt like she was wandering away from me, moving in Aimee's direction. What could I do though? I couldn't have stopped Dan going to Rhona's party.

If I'd stopped her…

Maybe she'd still be alive.

39

There Are More Snakes
Than Ladders

I woke up in the early hours of the morning. Not fully awake and never totally asleep, but anything was better than nothing these days. My mouth felt stodgy, so I staggered towards the landing where I followed my instincts towards the nearest tap. *Water*, my brain said, *cool drink of water*. My nightgown billowed like gossamer wings as I moved quietly, but quickly, downstairs towards the kitchen.

That's when I heard a noise in the night.

"Father?" I asked, my hands instinctively pulling the folds of my nightgown tightly over my body. But it wasn't a ghost that had made the noise. It was real. I heard it again.

TCR 01:03:26:42

I've been hearing a lot of funny noises in and around the old house recently. It's the strangest thing. They'll start, I'll listen, and they'll stop. Isn't that strange?

TCR 01:03:55:49

It was the distant scraping sound of wood against wood, but in the oppressive dark gloom of the kitchen…it was loud enough to reach my ears. There. *Again*.

The sound of silence had been broken by a drawer being opened somewhere near me.

My muscles tensed, rooting me to the floor, as I waited for another noise.

I heard nothing other than the sound of my chest heaving nervously.

My first instinct was to run upstairs and wake you up.

My second instinct, the one that conquered, was to investigate the invisible intruder.

I crept slowly out of the kitchen, moving towards where I thought I'd heard the intruding noise. When I entered the hallway, I saw a faint source of light coming from downstairs. My eyes widened in shock. There *was* someone downstairs!

And that's when I suddenly remembered we had Imelda staying with us.

My sluggish brain hadn't been thinking properly.

She was in the house, an intruder in our midst, and she was up to no good.

Bright light seeped out of the cracks in the door at the far side of the lower level of the house; it somehow didn't surprise me to see Imelda inside Father's Secret Cinema. Of course that's where she was lurking. Where else would she be? I couldn't imagine her digging for mealworms or mowing the field. The red door at the far end of the hall, the opposite side to The Secret Cinema, was locked, so Imelda couldn't be in that room.

She was looking for something in Father's personal domain.

I stood by the door and waited, holding my breath until the world whirled. Then I heard her voice. Frustration turned it into a hiss:

"There has to be a key or a file that'll lead me to his hidden bank accounts."

My heart shuddered at the sound of her voice. The world seemed to pause until I caught my breath. I felt sick but excited too. She wanted money but didn't know how to get it.

I remained outside the door; listening, hoping for more information.

"What did he say in his stupid message? Something about a locked box?"

She was literally having a conversation with herself.

"I'll get that money," her voice snarled, "and then I'll pay someone to build me a life-size dummy of The Deacon – so I can beat the crap out of it every night."

The sound of another drawer being closed – this time slammed in frustration – startled me so much that I backed away back into the hallway.

And accidentally collided with a vase on display.

My hands blurred and caught the vase before it collided with the carpet.

I'd heard enough. It was time to go back to bed. I replaced the vase and moved down the hallway, quickly up the stairs towards my bedroom.

A few minutes later, as I lay snugly with the quilt around me, I heard Imelda coming closer to me. The door creaked open slowly, slowly, slowly…

"Little Star," a voice said mockingly in the night.

I bit the side of my tongue until I tasted blood.

40

Unanswered Questions

My first reaction was to tell you all about Imelda's nocturnal trips around The Sanctum, but I had to be savvy about what I'd discovered. Besides, what would I tell you?

I didn't really know what she expected to find.

Secret bank accounts, evidently. So secret I didn't know about them.

Until then, I thought it best to keep quiet.

But I wouldn't give up until I knew the truth.

Besides, I had other distractions to keep me busy, one of which kept niggling away at the back of my mind; it was a single question, but an important one:

Whatever had happened to the letter Dan had asked me to deliver?

TCR 01:05:20:15

41

Every Day Is Like Monday, Tuesday, Wednesday, etc.

One day at Morvern High was the same as the next, bar a few minor differences. First period Mathematics was taught by Mr Bornstein, a nice little man who happened to be really dull. That's why everyone called him Mr Boringstein, but I quite liked him. He told me that all of life could be unlocked by equations.

I have an equation:

breakfast + poison = subtracted life.

Isn't that a neat formula? Second period was the domain of Miss Cromwell, my History teacher. "*Miss* Cromwell," Dan often mused in the same way she spoke of Aimee. "Why is she still a 'Miss'?" I couldn't answer that question. But I could tell that Miss Cromwell liked her angora sweaters. She had dozens of them in different colours, so Monday she wore green, Tuesday it was pink, Wednesday black, Thursday a nice mauve, and Friday white – the same colour as Gerard Way's hair during The Black Parade's promotional campaign. Who told me that? Dan did, of course.

Third period was English, courtesy of Mr Martens, whose face and surname reminded me of old boots. He was fine, though he kept talking about someone named Shakespeare. *'To be, or not to be...'* makes no sense to me.

Fourth period alternated between PE and Domestic Sciences. I think someone added *Science* to *Domestic* to make the class sound a bit fancy – less domestic.

Fifth period was Religious Education with Mr Taft, whose hair is definitely false. I know this because it fell off his head and landed on my arm during one lesson. Everyone laughed at me when I screamed and flicked the toupee away, propelling it across the room until it landed on Tracy Jack's shoulder.

Religious Education wasn't my favourite lesson because I'd spent an entire lifetime being taught about Sorak The Almighty. Instead of finding other religions interesting, I discovered they were actually all the same: a series of rules forbidding me to do anything and everything. Sometimes I wish the world could rid itself of religion.

But ridding it of religion would mean ridding it of people.

42

I've Got A Golden Tiiiicket!

It became my life's ambition to score an invitation to Rhona's birthday party. I did *everything* to gain her attention. 'Everything' included smiling at her in the corridor (she shouted "dyke" and ran off) and doing her English homework. All those extra points in my Vocab Test finally came in useful for something. She made me fetch her lunch and carry her books around the corridors of Morvern High; but don't think for a moment that I was a victim. I used her too. I'd have done *anything* for a ticket to Rhona's hallowed house party. It was all people talked about at the lockers.

According to the rumours, she had a Jacuzzi.

That isn't so impressive. We have a swimming pool. Father couldn't baptise converts in the river that runs through Glowglass Estate because it's so dirty. I'd rather not have my face anywhere near that grotty stream. In hindsight, Father had to build a swimming pool in the garden even if it cost a lot of money.

TCR 01:07:11:03

Anyway, it took three weeks of sucking up to the loathsome Rhona until she finally relented.

She took me aside at lunchtime after I'd stood in the queue for thirty minutes to get her the Diet Coke she wanted. Her hair was pinned up in an intricate design, which made my eyes wander, marvelling at the complexity. Not only did she have a Jacuzzi, it seemed Rhona had a personal hair stylist too.

"You really want to go to my birthday party, don't you?"

"YES!" I shouted.

She looked around, cringing in embarrassment. I didn't care.

I just wanted one thing.

"I'll put you on the guest list," she finally said, her voice low and reluctant.

It was all I could do not to dance and scream and weep and wail in hopeless joy.

"Is this the first party you've ever been invited to?"

"No," I said firmly, trying hard to pull myself together.

"This is *so* the first party you've been invited to!" Rhona chuckled.

She didn't understand. Okay, she was right. It *was* my first ever party. Parties were frowned upon by Father because any celebration that wasn't connected to Sorak was considered sinful. After all, didn't Sorak The Almighty have this to say about parties in Volume Three of his *Iconic Black Books*:

A little party never helped anyone get into Heaven.

But I figured there wouldn't be any harm in going to a party, if only to see what happened at them. Perhaps, I thought, there might be a way to bring people into the light of Sorak?

Delusional or what?

TCR 01:07:59:33

43

Dark Souls

Dan was slightly distant from me, but I didn't take it personally. It wasn't like she could totally replace me with Aimee. One day, during lunch break, we were leaning against one of Morvern High's cracked walls near the car park, tunelessly singing My Chemical Romance's *Planetary (GO!)*, when I suddenly realised that our duet had come to an unexpected end.

"What's wrong?" I asked tentatively.

Dan's eyes watered, the trails making tracks on her cheeks.

"I'm sick of keeping secrets," she answered.

I understood completely what she meant, so I told her one of my favourite quotes from Sorak The Almighty:

Secrets have a way of darkening your soul.

Dan chuckled then rubbed her face onto her sleeve, trying to make her face look the way it did before the wet streaks did their worst. I didn't mean my quote to sound so pompous, but I'd learned that sometimes – on occasion – Sorak The Almighty can give comfort to the uninitiated. If anyone knows about keeping secrets, it's me.

"Aimee and I aren't just friends," Dan explained.

"I know," I told her.

"You do?"

"I may be a bit naïve in some ways, but I'm adaptable."

"Did you learn that word for the Vocab Test?"

"Yes!"

We were silent for a few seconds, until Dan broke it with a smile and a compliment:

"I'm so glad you're going to Rhona's party."

"It was such a shock when Rhona asked me," I said shamelessly. "The invitation just came out of nowhere…"

Dan, to her credit, said nothing as we headed to our next lesson.

44

Sorak's Pen Is Mightier
Than Your Sword

Did you know that I once got to touch the actual *Iconic Black Books of Sorak The Almighty*? I didn't just get to hear about those books during our morning, evening and night-time prayer sessions. I'm one of the few initiates to have touched the pages with my fingertips, looked at the text with my eyes, and soaked up the history of our iconography!

You bought me a doll on my tenth birthday and told me to keep it secret.

But Father also asked me to keep a secret on my tenth birthday.

TCR 01:09:16:52

"This book," Father told me with blurry eyes, "has been passed down from generation to generation. My Father read it to me, just as his Father read it to him. And now I am reading it to you, a mere girl." He moved his withered hands across the thick black leather cover as though stroking a cat. "But it is your birthday, after all, and you're such a good disciple. I thought...why not?"

No words passed from between my lips, because I was too frightened to talk.

"You don't want to touch a book that Sorak Himself once held?"

Fear had turned me into a fool.

"I do!"

Satisfied with my eager reaction, Father lifted the first volume and opened it.

"This book contains the history of our Church. It was gifted to my grandfather by his grandfather for safekeeping after The War of Enlightenment. It is said that Sorak wrote the litany in his own blood, invocations of His will made manifest."

My eyes were transfixed on the book, because it held power with its pages.

The shabby tome was the most extraordinary thing I'd ever seen in my entire life. Could it really be that Sorak had touched those pages aeons ago?

There, in front of me, was proof of Sorak's existence.

It seemed scarcely believable and yet…

And yet to think otherwise would be the same as calling Father a liar.

Father was incapable of lying to me, or his other brethren.

Or so I'd been raised to believe. You too, but you weren't as gullible.

TCR 01:10:11:47

"Do you want to read it?" Father asked excitedly.

I couldn't breathe. This was the ultimate honour! Me, Starrsha Glowglass, the only girl in our Church, reading one of *The Iconic Black Books of Sorak The Almighty*?

"Yes," I replied, my voice quivering in anticipation.

My fingers passed over Father's gnarled hand, slowly but surely removing the book from his protective clutch. This was the most significant moment of my life, which wasn't saying much because my life, just like your life, consisted of rigid routine and constant prayer.

But on that birthday, I felt I could do anything.

I could dance.

I could fly.

I could…

I could see the truth for the first time in my life.

Something wasn't right.

"What's wrong, girl?" Father seemed irritated by my muted reaction.

"Nothing," I squeaked, not daring to look at him, finding solace in my feet.

"What is it? Don't lie to me child or the unending fury of Sorak's rage will burn you!"

Father's operatic voice hit the sort of notes that eunuchs could only dream of. "You *will* tell me," he screamed.

But I couldn't tell him. How could I reveal what I'd accidentally discovered? Only a lie saved me from his wrath.

"I'm truly excited to be reading the sacred words written down by Sorak," I said convincingly. My grin always seemed to bewitch Father. I was his favourite disciple, after all, one of the few members of our Family to sleep in The Sanctum rather than in the mill with everyone else. Father nodded, apparently satisfied with my explanation.

Then we resumed reading the *Iconic Black Books of Sorak The Almighty*.

TCR 01:11:02:19

Father never once suspected that I'd stumbled on the truth.

How could I tell him what the book had revealed to me?

How could I say that *I recognised Sorak's handwriting?*

Eventually, however, I told him that I knew all about his deception.

TCR 01:11:30:45

I blurted out the words over dinner, much to the horror of his three wives, each sitting around the table. You weren't there, of course. You'd been sent back to the mill and your dormitory to have dinner with the others.

"I know the truth about *The Iconic Black Books*."

"Child," he replied evenly, as though he'd prepared for the moment his entire life, "Sorak The Almighty works through my body. My hand is His hand. His handwriting is my handwriting. Do you not see that I am His voice and will on Earth?"

It seemed a reasonable excuse and one I eagerly seized upon.

A question: is it terrible that I wanted to believe him so much that I let his explanation override my instincts? I can't stop believing in Sorak, even though He's probably a lie.

I *need* help.

45

My First Party

The night of Rhona's party was stressful. Why? Because I had no idea how to dress for it. There wasn't a specific code, but my instincts told me not to dress in anything boring or 'churchy', which was the adjective most girls in the school corridors used to describe me. "Her dungarees are very churchy," or, "she needs to pray for better style."

There I stood in front of my full-length mirror, posing and planning, finding fault in everything I put on my body. The hang-ups I have about my appearance go back to my childhood brainwashing. It got so bad that I still shower in the dark.

A polite cough alerted me to the fact that I wasn't alone.

"I have some outfits you could wear to the party," said Aunt Imelda.

"No thank you," I replied firmly.

"What have you got to lose?"

"My dignity?"

"My dear," Imelda snickered, "you lost your dignity years ago."

The outfit I had didn't look very cool. It was a homemade tie-dye T-shirt all the colours of the rainbow, with a pair of white jeans. Somehow it just felt wrong. Worse, somewhere in my head a voice told me that Imelda was probably right.

"No strings attached?" I asked cautiously.

"I'm your auntie," Imelda said with a smile.

It wasn't a proper answer to my question, but desperation made my resolve weak. Imelda left my bedroom, only to return a few minutes later with clothes folded neatly on her forearm. They were a bit cheap and nasty, just like Imelda, but maybe something would make me stand out at the party.

Every time Imelda made a suggestion, I slapped it aside with two words:

"This is a micro mini skirt…"

"No. Next."

"If you put this belt around your chest, we can use tape to secure…"

"Absolutely never."

"How about this knee-length see-through PVC coat?"

"What? Next."

"You'll surely love this hot little crop top…"

"Burn it."

"You're more crash test dummy than shop window dummy," Imelda grumbled as she threw her pile of clothes onto my bed. Her hands seized, and then discarded, each item as I turned away from it. Eventually we settled on something that I felt comfortable enough wearing in public. Honestly, Imelda has the nastiest taste in clothing and Sorak would not approve at all. But there was also the matter of time, which was pressing on me to hurry up and get a taxi to Rhona's house.

First, I had to find you and see what you thought of my ensemble.

"How do I look?"

The expression on your face as you took in the sight of me wearing a **red** fluffy sweater, **yellow** denim hot pants, and **green** Converse sneakers was hilarious.

YOU LOOK LIKE YOU'LL STOP TRAFFIC, you said with a snort of laughter.

"I'm sure you'll have a night to remember," Imelda said as she waved me off. She was right, but for all the wrong reasons.

46

Booze Monks

Dan met me in a taxi cab on the way to Rhona's house. She seemed a bit tense, but did well to mask her growing uneasiness, which manifested itself on her skin as a rash of acne, buried under a light foundation. Apparently. Aimee had arranged to meet her on the way to the party, but had cancelled without explanation. But at least she had me and that mattered more than she'd ever know. I was terribly excited. My first party! This was the life I wanted now that Father had crossed over to the other side. I'd always wanted to be normal and here I was with my best friend, heading into town on a Friday night.

But my good mood was about to be violently punctured.

Unfortunately, the driver of our taxi recognised me.

TCR 01:13:36:03

"Hey," he gasped, "you're The Oatmeal Girl, aren't you?"

Dan's fingers self-consciously brushed against her face, thinking he was referring to her skin. She suddenly realised with a clear sense of relief that the driver was glaring at me from the rear-view mirror. His eyes were heavy and his brow thick with coarse dark hair.

"What was it like?"

"What?" I asked, trying with great difficulty to be polite.

"You know…seeing all that death in front of you?"

"Really, bitch?" Dan snapped irritably at the driver.

I tried to calm her before she punched him, but I was only partly successful.

"Here's what I think happened," the driver continued, ignoring my best friend. "I reckon old Deacon Glowglass knew the tax man was after him and he realised that his Church's charitable status would be scrapped and he'd owe millions…"

"We're self-sufficient," I explained tersely, reciting the speech I'd heard Father yell from the lectern many times in the past. "Our oatmeal is sold to companies who use it in their products. Our oatmeal is found in some of the famous brands—"

"Anyway," the driver said, cutting me off the way he did other drivers on the main road, "we all know the easiest way to avoid paying your taxes is to invent your own religion. Did you know all that stuff was guff?"

"Guff?" I asked, not quite understanding.

"It means bullshit," Dan explained helpfully. "It wouldn't do well in the Vocab Test."

Normally I would have laughed, but I had something to say:

"Our oatmeal is found in some of the famous brands of porridge," I tried again, "and the money we earn is used to fund our pursuit of Sorak's way of life—"

But I was cut off again by that power-drill voice behind the wheel.

"Have either of you two ever been to Devon? It's a lovely place, Devon."

TCR 01:14:13:41

It was round about this point of the conversation that I surrendered and let the driver speak without any resistance. Every time I attempted to say something, he butted in and said more ridiculous things.

He was a rude guff merchant. Guff, guff, guff, guff, GUFF.

"Devon is where those monks in Buckfast Abbey create that tonic wine that people drink and drink until they're drunk. Good men, those monks. They make loads of money from their product! Well...they earn it, but religion and big business aren't necessarily in opposition. Who would have thought that a few monks would end up with such a huge wine business?"

"I need wine after listening to you," Dan whispered from her side of the backseat.

My giggles were stifled by my fist, the knuckles of which I'd inserted into my mouth.

"I bet those monks have a lot of money stashed away in Devon," the driver said, whilst turning the wheel of his cab. "But then you probably have loads hidden somewhere in your house, far away from the taxman's fidgety fingers."

TCR 01:15:00:59

Not only do people think we're weirdo survivors of a mass suicide, they also believe we're secret millionaires. Maybe we're both. You'll know soon.

TCR 01:15:20:17

The journey to Rhona's house didn't take long. Ten minutes, slightly more. It was only after the loony driver ignored his second red light that I suddenly understood your joke about my outfit and 'stopping traffic'.

Ha!

47

My Last Party

The party wasn't just a disaster.

It was a damn tragedy.

How could I not have known it would turn out this way? Rhona seemed ridiculously happy when she answered the door to me and Dan. Her smile was genuine, but it wasn't worn for our benefit. It masked a private joke, something shared with her real friends. That smile was a code that I didn't crack until it was too late.

By then it was already too late.

TCR 01:16:12:38

"You have a lovely house," I said as Rhona gave me and Dan a tour of her home. The party was in full swing and I recognised faces from different classes at school. The loud music obliterated any attempt at meaningful conversation, so I tried to keep it light and fun. What did people do at parties anyway? But I already knew:

They got drunk.

As a Child of Sorak The Almighty, it was against everything I stood for to drink alcohol.

But…everyone else seemed to have a little green bottle in their hand.

"Hi Aimee!" Dan suddenly called out, her voice carrying successfully over the music.

I saw Aimee sitting in the corner with one of those green bottles in her hand. The neon light from a rather large aquarium mounted to the wall bathed her face in a pinkish glow. Beautiful and regal, it always wounded me to look at Aimee. I'd never be as pretty as her, or as popular, but I could be one thing she couldn't:

I'd always be Dan's best friend.

It turned out she wasn't even interested in being Dan's best friend, let alone her girlfriend. Aimee turned away from me and Dan, a raised eyebrow marring her beautiful features.

Dan's face crumbled in disappointment.

Suddenly the tone of the entire party altered; it was a subtle but noticeable shift.

It felt darker, even nasty.

"Is something wrong?" Rhona asked, her false eyelashes fluttering.

"No," Dan responded a little too quickly. "Why?"

"You look a little bit sad," Rhona laughed.

Yes, she actually *laughed* whilst uttering those words.

Before I knew it, someone had pressed a little green bottle into my right hand.

"Enjoy!" Rhona said as she watched me struggle with the lid.

Rhona stepped forward and took it off with her teeth.

That was the first time I'd ever tasted alcohol.

It was like drinking mouthwash but swallowing instead of spitting it out.

Why didn't I stop?

The rest of the night shot past me in a blur.

Even now I can't remember all of it.

TCR 01:16:49:25

I remember being with Dan and talking to her about *everything*.

For the first time in my life I was honest about what I'd been through. We talked about Sorak The Almighty, Father, our Church, the videotaped message he'd sent us, The Witchcraft Purges and Auntie Imelda.

I told her everything that I'm telling you right now.

And in return Dan told *me* everything.

She was in love with Aimee and thought Aimee loved her too.

But Aimee didn't want to disappoint anyone, which in itself was disappointing.

TCR 01:17:01:49

Some time passed at the party. It felt like hours, but it might only have been minutes. I remember opening my eyes to see Rhona posing in the middle of a crowd, waving something at the gaggle of friends. It was paper, a small square of it.

It looked familiar. Where had I seen it before?

Then I remembered.

It was Dan's secret letter to Aimee.

"I found your love letter, dyke," Rhona shouted, hollering with laughter.

Rhona had somehow laid her acrylic grip on Dan's letter.

How? She *had* to have gone through my bag. In PE? In another class?

Dan leapt to her feet with a loud and furious cry of anger and pain.

The punch she wanted to give the taxi driver earlier was, instead, thrown at Rhona.

Something else was thrown too – by me, in fact.

My little green bottle was empty, so it sailed through the air easily enough.

The compact glass grenade missed Rhona, but Dan's fist blurred and successfully made contact. Rhona fell over heavily and hard. Her body slammed into the wall, the impact causing her to howl in pain as her shoulder met a hard surface. The fighting brought everyone else out and things turned really nasty.

People crowded around Rhona to read the letter.

Their laughter drowned out even the sound of the music from inside the house.

But the cruellest cut was yet to come.

Surrounded by her peers, Aimee was forced to deny the entire thing.

Instead of being honest, she took the easy way out.

I will never ever forgive her for what she did that night.

TCR 01:19:37:29

"Dan's stalking me," Aimee announced in front of the entire party, which practically amounted to everyone at school. The chain of lockers on Monday morning would link this gossip in a circuit of conversation. The main topic of discussion at Morvern High would be Dan's letter to Aimee. No-one would believe the truth. Even in my state I knew Dan was about to be alienated for being herself. How is that fair?

Why is it always the outsider that's punished?

Dan did nothing wrong and yet everyone wanted to destroy her.

"Aimee?" Dan said pleadingly, begging for some back-up.

"I'm not a dyke," Aimee hissed, suddenly looking less beautiful than I remembered.

And that was the end of a not-so-glorious secret romance.

"Let's get out of here," Dan said quietly as she dragged me out of Rhona's house.

TCR 01:20:15:18

We walked down the street together, her weight comfortably supporting me, pulling and pushing my body in a bid to make it walk properly. I remember seeing a taxi arrive and the thick scent of leather seat as Dan rested me on it.

But I also have a fragment in my brain of Dan waving goodnight.

"I'm going back to the party," she slurred.

"You're worse than me," I retorted, suddenly feeling my brain fighting back against the boozy bath I'd willingly submerged it in. But my protests were futile – Dan was already on her way back up the road towards the noisy house in the distance.

The taxi – with a different driver – took me away from my best friend and all the way back to The Sanctum. Even then I knew instinctively I'd done something wrong in leaving Dan alone at that damn party.

TCR 01:21:51:42

Forty minutes later I arrived back at The Sanctum with the contents of my stomach splattered across Imelda's fluffy sweater. The journey and the sudden surge of sickness had joined forces to make me bring it all up. Imelda's expensive sweater was utterly ruined. It really annoyed her, so at least *something* good came of going to Rhona's horrible party.

<PAUSE>   << *REWIND* <<

98

TCR 01:21:51:42
TCR 01:20:15:18
TCR 01:16:12:38
TCR 01:15:20:17

\<PLAY>

The journey to Rhona's house didn't take long. Ten minutes, slightly more. It was only after the idiot driver ignored his second red light that I suddenly understood your joke about my outfit and 'stopping traffic'.

Ha!

>> FAST FORWARD >>

TCR 01:15:20:17
TCR 01:16:12:38
TCR 01:20:15:18
TCR 01:22:00:11

\<PLAY>

Thank you for paying the fare. I forgot to thank you at the time.

I wish I'd pushed that first little green bottle away from me when it was offered. I'd go back and relive that entire night differently.

I wonder what would have happened if I'd remained sober.

Could I have stopped the fight before it started?

Could I have made sure Dan got into the taxi with me?

Could I have saved her life?

48

Who Put The *Fun* Into Funeral?

A teenage girl went out to a party and didn't come back home.

Here's what happened while I was throwing up in the back of a taxi. Dan, my best friend, staggered back towards Rhona's party, drunk and unsteady, only to be locked out of the house in the freezing cold. Her mind sluggish, but still able to move her legs, she stumbled away, faltering around until she collapsed next to a tree in Rhona's garden.

She fell asleep and froze to death.

It might sound like a stupid and senseless way to die, but let's not forget that Father supposedly poisoned our entire congregation with killer porridge.

What's more senseless than death by oatmeal?

TCR 01:23:47:32

Dan's parents buried her just over a week later in the same graveyard as her Gran and Grandfather. But she wasn't Dan; she was *Danielle*, a girl I'd never met in my life. Burying *Danielle* next to her grandparents made her folks feel better about what happened, though not much better. How could they feel anything other than utter confusion and crawling horror? But their daughter now had two people looking after her in Heaven, which seemed like small comfort for devastated parents.

The funeral itself left me cold and dare I say it...unfulfilled.

I sat in the middle of the church, a creaky wooden bench beneath my butt. Three songs were played, each chosen by Dan's folks – but none sounded like the sort of songs Dan would ever have put on any of her Spotify playlists. She didn't like Sam Smith, for a start. He sounds like a cat being throttled by its own whiskers. What happened to the My Chemical Romance songs? What about her other favourite bands like Real Friends or Taking Back Sunday? They weren't just bands to Dan – they were T-shirts, posters, identity, inspiration, and her shield against conformism.

TCR 01:24:15:19

One of the headlines in the aftermath of Dan's death reduced me to rubble. It read:

"EMO TEEN DEAD AFTER BOOZY NIGHT OUT GOES WRONG"

The article referenced a 'sinister trend of Emo fans romanticising death," blah blah blah.

I read the story over and over again, hoping it would make sense. It did not.

TCR 01:24:52:59

Dan's parents had her coffin propped up, lid open, in their living room for a week before the funeral. Her hair wasn't sitting right. It had been styled wrongly. How couldn't they see how bad it looked? Wasn't anyone paying attention? Oh, I wanted to reach into the coffin and fix Dan's hair.

At one point during the funeral, a man in white robes entered the church to a hymn. He swung a chain with a jar of incense. The syrupy smell overwhelmed me and I gagged. It took me all of my self-control to stifle the sneeze that tickled my nose and throat.

The only place Dan lives is in our memories. From time to time I visit my friend by thinking about the fun we had and how much she helped me at Morvern High.

I'm about to start crying again. Let me get a grip of myself.

TCR 01:27:59:30

Okay. I'm back.

Sorak The Almighty had this to say about death:

Four things in this world are inevitable: life, death, taxes and false teeth.

Truly, Sorak is a wise deity. In all honesty, I prefer our way of seeing people off to the other side. Whenever someone from The Church of Sorak passes away – and that's all of them except us – our memorial service is a lot different to what I experienced at Dan's funeral. For a start, we sing songs of praise. One song that I've always particularly enjoyed singing is a composition called *Imagine* – and I feel like singing it right now.

Forgive me, but I don't have a piano and it always sounds better with a piano:

> *Imagine there's no Sorak*
> *It's enough to make you cry*
> *Pure hell around us*
> *Any moment we could die*
> *Imagine all the people*
> *Living for Sorak… Aha-ah…*
>
> *Imagine there's no oatmeal*
> *What the heck would we do?*
> *Nothing to work or live for*
> *And high taxes, too*
> *Imagine all the people*
> *Living life in sin… Ooooh…*
>
> *You may say I'm a dreamer*
> *But I'm not the only one…*

Well, you get the idea.

Father claimed he wrote this song one night after Sorak The Almighty sent him a divine vision. Not only did he love classic-era Hollywood movies, but I reckon the old Deacon was a thwarted rock star too. Any excuse for him to get out his guitar and strum a tune!

After the Day Of The Final Prayer (I'll get to *that* in due course) we held our own little remembrance ceremony to celebrate the lives of our Family. You can't sing because you can't speak, of course. But I performed the song and felt so proud afterwards.

And then I heard John Lennon's *Imagine* for the first time in Boomania with Dan.

Yes. Father ripped off a Beatle for his crappy song.

We scattered the ashes of our brothers and sisters to a stolen song.

49

Hand Chatter

The first day back at school without Dan was horrible. Not one person spoke to me. They didn't care enough for my feelings to ask about them. Between us, it was a relief because I didn't want to talk about Dan's death anyway.

I found you and Aunt Imelda in the kitchen waiting for me to arrive home from school. The expression on your face, different from that of Imelda's smirk, alerted me to the fact that something bad had happened.

Imelda slowly raised her hand to show me the cause of the bad atmosphere. Another black video cassette. A new one.

THIS ARRIVED BY POST THIS MORNING, you said slowly.

"Have you watched it yet?" I asked.

"We thought it would be better to wait until you got back," said Imelda

"How thoughtful of you," I said to Imelda, but my tone was sour.

"There's something else." Imelda motioned to the kitchen table.

My eyes followed her hand until they stopped at a small white box.

You moved your fingers until they formed a sentence:

AFTER WHAT HAPPENED TO YOUR FRIEND, I WANT TO MAKE SURE YOU'RE ALWAYS IN CONTACT WITH ME AND IMELDA.

Inside the little white box was my very first iPhone.

TCR 01:29:58:12

I'd noticed everyone at school talking into their hands, not looking at each other, but talking in their own way. Father had banned phones from the church grounds, except the one he had stashed away in his Secret Cinema. Old hypocrite. I felt I didn't need a phone.

Besides, I didn't have any friends, so no phone numbers to ask for.

Grateful that you cared so much, I asked:

"Could I speak to you before we head downstairs?"

Then, for the avoidance of doubt, I added: "In private."

Imelda raised a dark eyebrow, and then stood up from her chair, revealing her latest outfit, which was basically...*SIGH*...a tiny pink bikini with a pair of matching heels. I bristled with fury as she passed me and exited the kitchen. You shrugged your shoulders instead of spelling with your fingers, but I understood the meaning.

"I don't want her here," I said firmly.

WE HAVE NO CHOICE. FATHER WANTED HER BACK IN THE FAMILY HOME. WE HAVE TO WAIT AND SEE HOW IT PANS OUT.

"I don't trust her."

SHE DOESN'T TRUST YOU EITHER, NOT AFTER YOU STOLE SOME OF HER CLOTHES FOR THAT PARTY.

What you said didn't make sense to me, not at first.

Then the meaning became apparent.

I screamed like Godzilla with a gobstopper stuck in his throat:

"That cow!" I seethed. "She loaned me her sweater and shorts for the party! I nearly ended up dying of hypothermia like my best friend; it was that cold outside."

SHE SAID YOU STOLE THEM—FROM HER BEDROOM CUPBOARD.

"Rotten backstabbing guff queen," I wailed.

Anger made me careless, so I told you what I knew about Auntie:

"She was sneaking about downstairs a fortnight ago."

You didn't seem too surprised, to give you a little credit.

"She's here on some sort of mission. I think she's after something here in The Sanctum, possibly in The Secret Cinema."

WHAT COULD SHE BE LOOKING FOR?

I paused, thinking about it seriously, then said:

"I think she's after The Deacon's money."

TCR 01:30:51:39

105

50

The Second Message

Together we headed downstairs to The Secret Cinema, where the only VCR in the entire house, possibly in Morvern itself, could be found. Imelda was already there, sitting on the black leather chair Father enjoyed sitting on when he watched his movies.

I looked at my Auntie with hatred in my heart.

She returned my look with a defiant smirk.

Imelda couldn't stay out of my way. She had to shove herself in my face. She was as ubiquitous as Elton John at a celebrity funeral. Why couldn't she just leave us alone?

You waved the new video cassette in our faces.

ARE WE READY?

My voice came out as a whine: "Do we really need to?"

"Yes," Imelda cried out with glittery eyes, "do it now!"

You slid the tape into the VCR.

Once again our TV brought Father back from the dead in surround-sound stereo.

01:32:04:19

"If everything is proceeding to Sorak The Almighty's plan, then my ghastly younger sister should be there in The Sanctum with all of you. I hope you're being nice to her."

I frowned. You noticed it. But Father seemed to believe that he alone was going to die. It was in the words he used: did he honestly think everyone else would be with us watching the tape. Was that the mentality of a man who plotted a mass murder suicide of his entire congregation? No. He knew he was in danger, but he didn't realise everyone in the congregation would pay the price for his evil. And here he was, speaking again.

How could one dead man be such a pest?

"Imelda!" Father shouted, his voice booming from the speakers. *"Imelda!"*

"I'm here, old git."

It was as though they were having a proper conversation with each other.

"You are one of the most vile and repulsive traitors to our Church that I have ever had the misfortune to come across. You refuse penance and revel in your grotesque sinful ways. You have been with too many men and you wear unseemly attire!"

Between us, I was absolutely living for the *roasting* Imelda was receiving from the TV.

"You returned not out of obligation to our cause, but because you want my money! Yes, I've said it. I have money hidden away. But you won't get your hands on it. You are not worthy enough. My followers are here and they will stop you. Your brothers and sisters will laugh as you fail to find my fortune."

"Your followers followed you to Hell," Imelda cracked.

"Disrespectful," I said firmly.

"I'm being verbally violated by a ghost in a videotape."

Father wasn't quite finished yet. He had prepared another nasty surprise for us.

"I have something important to announce to my congregation!"

AND HERE IT COMES, you said.

"There is another visitor on their way to our church."

Imelda's eyes widened in…was it fear?

"He is returning," Father screeched.

OH NO.

"*Who* is returning?" I asked, but you seemed too startled to respond.

Father answered my question from inside the television:

"Please give your Uncle Ezra my warmest regards," he said gleefully.

Imelda stood up, uttered a long shrieking scream, and fled the room.

"I think that went really well," I said sarcastically.

51

Death Is Confusion

School was my escape from the lunacy within the four walls, but it wasn't an ideal place for me, especially after what happened to Dan. My classmates were astonished to discover someone they saw every day, someone they knew, could be there one day and then…gone. Death is confusion. Nothing ever feels quite right afterwards. Life seems normal, but there's a gap shaped like a person in your world and no-one else can fit comfortably into that same space. People who have suffered loss understand what I'm saying: they still do the things you normally did before that person died; they talk and work and sometimes they even laugh – but they do it all with less certainty.

TCR 01:34:18:44

Aimee would, on occasion, cross the schoolyard with purpose in her step. But the closer she came to me, the more her resolve withered. What did she want anyway? Did she intend to apologise for being gutless at Rhona's party? Or did she want to talk about Dan? Maybe she wanted to tell me what happened to Dan after I got into that taxi?

Maybe.

But she never got the chance.

Sorak The Almighty has a quote for the likes of Aimee Curtis:

Evil can't harm you unless you let it.

I'd never ever speak to her as long as I had the use of my legs to move me into another room. That applied to Rhona as well. They made my skin crawl, both as bad as each other, never happy unless they were scheming and ruining lives.

My spare time was spent praying to Sorak The Almighty for help and guidance. Imelda found this hilariously funny, and she'd laugh as I prayed for a sign of Sorak's glory. Her words could not touch me. I'd pray zealously in the morning, evening and just before I headed to bed. But my prayers went unanswered for a few weeks until…well… how do I say this without sounding nuts?

Until I received a phone call from Heaven.

52

The Day Sorak Went Cuckoo Doodle Doo

I'll never forget the day Sorak went cuckoo doodle doo, because it was mostly like any normal day except for me having *forty-two* missed calls on my fancy new iPhone. Now, you might wonder how Sorak The Almighty got a hold of my number, but Sorak is all-knowing, all-seeing and all-powerful. Are you really that surprised that He has a really strong signal in Heaven? Maybe there are phone masts up in the sky that we can't see? Yes, my phone was connected to Heaven's hotline.

Sorak's voice wasn't quite what I expected it to be either.

There was a duality in the voice that made it hard to pin down a specific accent or a gender. Sorak's voice sounded like a mixture of many different things. It was male and female, strong and soft, happy and sad...but most of all the voice was sane and insane.

It was a frightening voice but oddly beautiful at the same time.

This is what happened as I remember:

TCR 01:36:30:19

It was in the middle of Religious Education that I realised my satchel was buzzing gently on the floor by my feet. My iPhone had been set to SILENT MODE, though not by me. Honestly, I didn't really want a phone. Don't think I'm being ungrateful for your present, but I was frightened of becoming one of those teenage zombies that stalked Morvern High, shuffling slowly around the schoolyard, eyes fixed on a little screen in my hand. The phone felt like it might slowly change me into a zombie.

But the buzzing wouldn't stop.

Mr Taft looked at me and his wig shifted on his scalp.

"Sorry," I mumbled, but he continued his lesson and left me alone.

I reached into my satchel, felt for the phone, and raised it into the light: *42 MISSED CALLS.*

"What?" I cried out, before raising my hand across my mouth.

Mr Taft continued his speech about Stephen Fry and his blasphemous ways.

Who would want to call *me* forty-two times?

I slumped over in my chair and found myself sinking deeper and deeper into depression.

TCR 01:37:43:22

The caller managed to get me on his forty-third attempt. I was between classes and no-one paid attention to me in the bustling corridors as I fidgeted with the little screen in my hand. This was my first ever call on my brand-new iPhone. Why wasn't I more excited? Perhaps because I'd always imagined it would be Dan at the other end of my first ever phone call?

"Hello," I said to my mysterious caller.

"Starrsha," the voice echoed faintly from the receiver, *"is that you?"*

"Yes. Who is this?"

"It's me!"

The voice sounded slightly amused, as though it couldn't believe I didn't know its identity.

"Who?" I tried again.

"Sorak The Almighty!"

My fingers tightened around the iPhone until my knuckles hurt.

Honestly, it was the single creepiest moment in a life.

"You have been a good and faithful devotee of my cause," Sorak said in a tuneful voice, *"but you should have passed over with the rest of your family."*

"You're a foul piece of work, Imelda!"

Who else could it be?

"This is not Imelda."

"Okay. Rhona."

"I'm Sorak The Almighty and I'm having a bad day."

111

Is it possible for a god to have a bad day? I'll have to ask Mr Taft that question.

"Why is your day so bad?" I squeaked. Yes, I was having a conversation with Sorak.

"My day is bad because you've been bad."

"Really?"

"You haven't fulfilled your destiny."

"Okay. Let's pretend I believe you're Sorak The Almighty. What do you want?"

But I already knew what Sorak wanted. I just *knew*. He didn't disappoint me.

"You must go home and eat your porridge," the voice wailed all the way from Heaven.

"My...porridge?"

"Eat it up!"

"Can I put sugar in it?"

"Salt, my dear lost child. It must be salt."

Then:

"Add a little something extra to make the porridge taste all sour and delicious."

I dropped the phone and watched it fall to the floor.

It bounced once, twice, and landed.

Unfortunately, the hard-plastic shell was durable and didn't crack.

The special ingredient Sorak The Almighty had mentioned in his call to me?

Insecticide.

But you know that, don't you?

53

Santo Clowes

Have you ever stopped to consider how insane it is to spend your life in the service of someone you can't see and won't ever know? We love Sorak The Almighty and value His influence in our lives, even if we both question it from time to time. I suppose putting your faith in someone you'll never see isn't so weird. People outside the four walls believe in mystical figures they can't prove ever existed. For instance, Dan once told me all about someone named Santa Claus. He's a big guy with a red suit who travels across the world in twenty-four hours delivering presents to all children everywhere. As far as I can make out, Santa Claus is a benevolent figure who wants to make people happy. He does nice things for the sake of it. And in doing nice things for everyone, Santa is an inspirational figure for everyone else to do nice things too. The sad twist in this tale is that Santa Claus *is a lie told by parents to their children*. What sort of responsible adult does that to their kids?

It's **so** cruel. It shouldn't be allowed.

Disciples of Sorak don't have Santa Claus, but funnily enough we do have **Santo Clowes**.

Santo Clowes is a bit like Santa Claus, except he *takes* presents instead of giving them out. Haven't we enjoyed our Cristo Mass every year in December? The sheer exhilaration of giving presents to each other, and then handing them back to Father in honour of Santo Clowes...well, some of my favourite childhood memories are of those wonderful nights.

Sorak The Almighty said this of Cristo Mass:

If you don't believe, you won't receive.

And this, of course:

Only the truly sinful keep their presents from Santo Clowes!

In hindsight, it's understandable that some people might think Santo Clowes is a calculated Santa Claus copycat, another *Imagine*, but we'll never know for sure.

It does beg one important question that I've attempted to answer:

Where did our presents really go after we handed them over to Father?

There's a place online, a special place I discovered by accident.

It's called eBay and I reckon Father might have used it from time to time.

What *is* eBay? It's like the afterlife except unwanted gifts go there instead of souls.

Santo Clowes probably owns eBay, come to think of it.

54

Lost, Stressed And Depressed

Why didn't I tell you about Sorak The Almighty's crazy phone call? I didn't want to worry you. That's the simple excuse. The other excuse is that I was worried I'd imagined it. Did it really happen? Shortly after that first call, I walked out of school in a daze, not knowing if my sanity had shattered under the pressure. There's only so much a person can lose before finally losing their grip on reality.

I'd lost Dan. I'd lost my family. I'd lost everything.

Everything except you.

What would I do if you weren't here for me?

Thinking of everything I'd lost makes me remember my old life.

TCR 01:40:11:03

55

Linden's Hands Take A Trip

There were twenty-five members of The Family and I can name every one of them without pausing for breath.

They are Deacon Randolph William Glowglass, Mama Sadie, Mama Dora, Mama Esther, Kenneth, Milly, Linden, Mary-Beth, Joanie, Celestine, Pavel, Jacob, Ethan, Beki, Kimberley, Emir, Indigo, Morag, Dorinda, Rory, Tahir, Bryce, me and you. I miss having all that noise and life within the four walls. We ate, slept, prayed and worked together until The Morning Of The Final Prayer.

I miss all of them so much.

Well...nearly all of them.

TCR 01:41:05:49

On the rare occasions that Father left the confines of The Sanctum for a spiritual pilgrimage, he made certain his second-in-command remained behind to keep the church – and the oatmeal production lines – running smoothly. Brother Linden was Father's snivelling, weak-willed and willing protégé. Your bedroom used to belong to Linden. Yes, he was allowed to sleep in The Sanctum too. One of the newest additions to our Family, he arrived only a few years ago, on the run and looking for protection. He found peace in the loving embrace of Sorak The Almighty.

I know you didn't like Linden, but he was always okay with me. I found him a tad pathetic actually. But he *was* our Brother, so we had to tolerate his stupid behaviour even if we disagreed with it.

That meant the girls had to accept his wandering hands in silence.

Sister Dorinda particularly loathed him. She was one of the few people to speak out against Father if she felt he was pushing us too hard in the factory. He

116

punished her on occasion – tied her to a post, stripped, so we could spit on her one at a time, his way of making her readjust her attitude. Why did we stand for it? We should have said NO.

TCR 01:42:55:35

Linden, however, was no match for Dorinda, especially when Father wasn't around.

"Get lost," she shouted whenever Linden asked her to accompany him to a private prayer session. "What do you think I am?"

"You're a part of my flock," Linden would mumble, face bright with embarrassment.

"I'm part of Father's flock," Dorinda yelled back, as fiery as the freckles on her pale skin. "And he'd take a very dim view of what you're trying to do to me."

Ah, Dorinda. She was clever enough to make sure everyone knew what Linden was up to and never allowed herself to be alone in the same room with him.

I wish I'd done the same.

TCR 01:43:15:19

Linden absolutely lived for Father's religious pilgrimages, because he knew there would be no-one around to challenge his authority. As Father's protégé, he learned from the best…or should that be the worst? But not even Linden was prepared for the consequences of the really bad decision that cost him his crumb of power in our Church.

One day his hands wandered until they found the wrong person.

TCR 01:43:28:59

It happened during a lesson with Miss Gibson, my beautiful tutor. We were at the kitchen table with Linden in place of Father, keeping an eye on me for signs of rebellion. But the only rebellion taking place was an impromptu poetry lesson. We were meant to be learning arithmetic, but Miss Gibson – beautiful and faultless in a way Aimee Curtis could never match – decided my real education could start in Father's absence. We were halfway through writing my first sonnet (it stunk) when Linden reached out and stroked Miss Gibson's chestnut coloured hair. He actually touched her without asking!

Miss Gibson stiffened in shock. Her face, however, showed the unmistakable early warning signs of anger: narrow eyes, furrowed brow and tight pursed lips.

"Such a pretty lady," Linden sighed softly, his voice heavy with longing.

"I love it when someone touches me without permission," Miss Gibson said in a voice that didn't match the expression on her face, "because it means I can touch them too."

Linden smiled dopily; delighted she hadn't rejected him outright.

His dopy smile turned into a scream when Miss Gibson punched him hard between his legs. He howled and dropped to the floor, rolling uncontrollably as pain conquered him. Miss Gibson leapt off her chair and stamped down on him, performing a grotesque tap-dance. While she re-enacted *Riverdance* on Linden's face, I found myself thinking of another iconic quote from Sorak The Almighty:

If you're big enough to hit someone, you're big enough to be hit back.

Father went mad when he returned from his holy pilgrimage. He found it intolerable that Linden had tried his luck with an outsider, a guest not versed in the ways of Sorak. Father was petrified that Miss Gibson would tell the authorities what had happened, and that they would investigate his business affairs.

Miss Gibson was paid off and my tutoring sessions came to a hasty end.

And Linden?

The last I saw of his wandering hands, they were reaching out to me for help.

56
Simon Smiles

The one benefit of having the threat of Uncle Ezra hanging over us was that Imelda kept to herself. She wanted to leave, of course, but then she wouldn't be able to get her hands on the money she desperately wanted. She had two clear choices: leave The Sanctum and remain without the money, or remain in The Sanctum and leave with the money. But she wasn't happy at the prospect of being near her brother. It was exciting to know that someone could put Imelda in her place. What was this Ezra like? What power did he have? I wanted to know him. I hoped he'd like me.

Imelda's withdrawal, and Dan's death, effectively reset the balance of our world.

You sent a smile my way whenever we passed each other in The Sanctum.

Everything was better when you smiled.

Everything except school. Not even you could make that better for me.

TCR 01:45:35:31

57

Fashion Fiend

This is the point in my story where I introduce Cassie Trendy.

Who is Cassie Trendy? She's...well...a fashion fiend. Cassie Trendy – real name Cassandra Louella Trent – is the sort of girl who should have been laughed at by everyone. She wears enormous wigs, impossibly high-heeled shoes, and outrageous homemade outfits. She's more Marilyn Monroe than Marilyn Manson.

We *should* have laughed at Cassie. Instead we kissed her ass. Why? Because she's internet famous: Cassie has a YouTube channel; she is what people my age refer to as a 'Vlogger'. Her only show *I'm Trendy* is watched by thousands of people from all over the world.

Cassie has a special gift: an uncanny ability to spot what's cool before anyone else. And if she can't find anything exciting to write about, she randomly proclaims something to be cool – and suddenly it *becomes* cool. Her live broadcasts, beamed direct from her garage, are watched and dissected by her fans – tween girls who copy her style and affected mannerisms.

They want her clothes, her make-up tips and her wisdom.

TCR 01:46:12:49

Everything I know about Cassie came from Dan, told in that precious first week of our friendship when everything was thrilling and fresh.

According to my departed bestie, Cassie suffered from a rare psychological condition known as Rich Kids of Beverley Hills Syndrome, a non-fatal ailment that affects only one in every hundred teenagers. Sufferers find modesty an impossibility. The afflicted know *everything* about anything. No matter how much money you have, they always have more. If you won an Oscar for Best Actress or Actor, they would show off their trophy for Best Director.

Your car isn't as good as their private jet. Do you understand what I'm saying?

TCR 01:46:59:02

Cassie found me in the school library during one of my study periods. She was adorned in an oversized purple cape dress bearing psychedelic patterns. It was so ugly that not even I wanted to copy it in order to fit in with the cool girls.

The stress of being near someone as socially powerful at Morvern as Cassie made me anxious and mistrustful. After what happened at Rhona's party, can you blame me?

"Starrsha," Cassie purred, "it's *so* good to see you even though your shoes are vile."

"But you wore the same type of shoes a few weeks ago!"

"They're out of date, out of touch, out of time. A bit like you, Oatmeal Brain."

It took every tiny iota of my self-will to stop my fist from cracking her jaw and ruining her perfect pout – the same pout copied by thousands of fans worldwide.

However, her hatred for my shoes was the prelude to a silly question:

"Do you know what a yearbook is, Starrsha?"

"It's a photo album with pictures of everyone at school."

"Wrong!" Cassie Trendy shouted, her hands slamming down hard on the table. People angrily looked up in our direction. We were interrupting their precious study-time. But Cassie simply glared back at them until they melted beneath her gaze.

"A school yearbook is a portal into the past."

Yes, she uttered those exact words.

"And we need your help for the forthcoming yearbook."

I uttered the same sound that everyone in our Church made a few minutes after they ate their poisoned porridge: a guttural spluttering.

"How can I possibly help?" I gasped, whilst pulling away from the intruder at the table.

"We want to have a section dedicated to Danielle," Cassie explained, warming to her subject. "It'll be tasteful and stylish because *I'm* in charge of it."

Her hands pulled some photographs from a manila envelope and thrust them across the table until they were beneath my eyeline.

"No," I said. "They aren't suitable."

Cassie Trendy scowled. As a result, scowling suddenly became fashionable everywhere.

"Why not?"

"Those photographs are old. Dan's hair probably changed at least ten times after those were taken. If you're going to pay tribute to Dan, then it has to be respectful of the girl she became, the girl she wanted everyone to see…the girl I knew best."

Cassie nodded agreeably, suddenly realising that I could in fact prove useful in her plans.

"I'm so glad I consulted you," Cassie said with a flick of her platinum hair.

"Who else is helping with this tribute?"

"Aimee…"

"No," I snarled.

"Excuse me?"

"No!"

"Why not?"

"She put a knife deep in Dan's back. I won't forgive her!"

"EEK," Cassie Trendy squealed, her gossip radar pinging. "Tell me everything."

I didn't tell her everything, of course, but I told her enough.

"Let me get this *straight*, if you pardon the pun. Cactus Crotch was secretly dating Dan until a secret letter you were entrusted with fell into Rhona's hands. This led to Rhona humiliating Dan at a party – which I didn't get an invite to, so clearly it wasn't a cool party – and then Dan went back later, utterly drunk, to confront Aimee, only to be locked out in the cold where she later died of hypothermia?"

"Cactus Crotch?" I shrieked.

More students looked up at us with angry expressions.

"That's what I call Aimee. It's well-deserved, my dear. She spread a rumour that I suffer from Rich Kids of Beverley Hills Syndrome, which is preposterous."

"Aimee may have said something to a mutual friend about that," I said.

122

Cassie Trendy seemed to shift her attention away from Aimee and back to the manila envelope. "What else should we have in the yearbook as part of our tribute?"

"I'd like to write something for her, as a tribute to my friend."

"That's nice," Cassie Trendy exclaimed. "Oh yes I like that a lot."

There was one last thing I wanted to put in the yearbook.

"Could we have a photograph of Gerard Way in there too?"

Her face suddenly went the same colour as a block of sour cheese. Clearly Gerard was too odd for her musical palette. But before I could explain his significance in Dan's life, I felt the gentle tremble of my satchel from the floor as something inside it vibrated.

Someone was desperately trying to reach me on the phone.

I answered it, of course.

"Hello?"

"Go back to The Sanctum at once," Sorak The Almighty whispered from the other side.

"Why?"

"Because your uncle has arrived," Sorak said.

Then He added:

"And because I command it."

The call ended with a bleep and a tone.

TCR 01:48:35:07

58

The Second Visitor

Uncle Ezra wasn't quite what I'd expected. I found him in the study, comfortably perched on Father's large old leather chair, drinking tea and warming his hands by the fireplace.

Except there was no fire burning in the hearth.

"This fire is nice and warm," he said happily. "Perfect for the cold weather."

"But there's no fire…"

There was nothing more I could say to a man warming himself in an empty fireplace.

Ezra peered around the chair at me, frowning with noticeable confusion. His sunken face was round and flabby, while his eyes gleamed with mischief and fun. Sitting in front of me on the leather armchair was a man who apparently embodied all the qualities lacking in my Father; where Father's eyes were unfriendly and suspicious, his brother's eyes twinkled with jovial benevolence. Father only seemed to smile when we all ate our porridge, and he died with a rictus grin on his face after eating *his* porridge. Uncle Ezra, however, looked ruddy and red, the surface of his skin cracked with tiny thin veins. His was the face of a man who had travelled and who enjoyed the good things in life.

TCR 01:48:56:59

"Young lady," Uncle Ezra muttered, "I assure you that I have a lovely hot fire burning in front of me. I can feel the heat from the top of my toes to the tip of my nose."

"And I assure you, Uncle Ezra, that there's no fire burning right now."

Uncle Ezra leaned over and slowly pushed his right hand towards the fireplace, wiggling his fingers experimentally along the way. Then he pulled his hand back with a sudden burst of speed that belied his rotund appearance.

"Are you sure?"

"Yes!"

"So, if I reach into this fireplace, nothing will happen to me?"

"Nothing," I smiled benignly. He was utterly enchanting.

Uncle Ezra pushed his right-hand outwards, until it was deep in the fireplace.

Nothing happened.

Not at first.

Then Uncle Ezra screamed so loudly that my heart somersaulted in fright.

He pulled his hand away and clutched it in terrible pain, as though he really had just burned his hand in a fire. It was such a convincing performance that I almost found myself believing him.

"Stupid little bitch!" Uncle Ezra yelled as tears poured down his face. "Stupid ignorant wilful little hag! You did that on purpose. What sort of girl would stand by as a helpless old man burned himself in a fire?"

The ferocity of his anger and hurt startled me. It wasn't what I'd expected from a seemingly dotty old pensioner. But Uncle Ezra was anything but old and feeble. He was fast, and he was on his feet before I could flee the study, swiftly crossing the length of the room to reach me. His left hand snatched the fireplace poker along the way.

I darted to the study door that I'd entered a few moments beforehand.

It was closed tightly shut.

"What?!" I cried out in confusion.

My hand frantically tugged on the ornate brass handle only to find resistance.

Someone had locked the door from the other side!

"Imelda!" I screamed. "Simon!"

The only sound I heard was the muffled snort of an evil little laugh.

Hot breath brushed the hairs on my neck and slowly, very slowly, I turned around.

Uncle Ezra stood facing me, with the poker wavering over his head.

"There is evil in your heart."

I fell backwards, sliding down the door until the rough shabby carpet was beneath me.

"I will beat the evil out of you."

The poker smashed down on me once…twice…three times…until…

Until I lost count and blacked out.

59

Rolling In The Bleep Bleep Bleep

Here's an inventory of all the injuries I sustained as a result of Uncle Ezra's beating:

Firstly, he fractured my skull. He could have battered my brains out onto the carpet – he nearly did – but I managed to throw my hands up and protect myself from the worst of his volley. I still suffer from headaches as a result of Uncle Ezra's attack. My headaches sound like horrible music, they ring loud in my ears. Sometimes I remember situations one way, sometimes another. My skull is a scrambled egg. It was a 'basal fracture' according to the nice doctor in the ward. Do you know that a basal fracture is the worst kind of fractured skull you can suffer?

Do you know what else the nice doctor said while I lay helpless in a hospital bed, hooked up to The Bleeping Machine? He said, "Oh you're very lucky to have survived that nasty fall. That'll teach you to send a text while walking down a staircase." Did Imelda concoct that stupid story? Or perhaps you didn't want to bring the police back into The Sanctum again? Maybe you said it to protect Crazy Uncle Ezra from facing up to what he did?

But he didn't do it alone.

Someone was outside that door.

And they enjoyed the sounds of screaming girl and scrambling skull.

TCR 01:50:05:27

Those few months were awkward for me because I never felt welcome in the hospital. It wasn't personal, not like at school, but the staff really needed my bed and I wasn't quite ready to go home. At one point, early one morning, my bed was moved into the corridor because someone else wanted the room. There I lay, still and frightened, unable to protest or move as indignity after indignity was heaped upon me. At one point a young girl started taking selfies with me. I pretended to be asleep. It was better than having to look at people walking past me, like they did in the school corridors.

"Look," the girl with the phone said to someone nearby. "Do you think she's dead?"

A hand lifted up my wrist, which I allowed to droop limp and useless.

"Put that down," another voice hissed, probably the girl's mother.

"I'm taking a selfie," the girl replied.

Between us, I wanted to slap the brat.

The girl had taken a lot of photographs of me as I lay motionless, while the conversation between her and her mother took place right beside me.

"I wonder how she died," the little girl said thoughtfully.

"Boredom," I croaked in the spookiest voice I could muster.

The girl and her mother screamed in fright. Then the woman shouted at me for upsetting her daughter. Soon enough a nurse came and put me back in my room, where I lay alone for what felt like forever. Forever isn't *so* long if people visit you in hospital.

Two people I didn't expect to see came to visit me.

60

A Trendy Guest

The first visitor was Cassie Trendy, which was a surprise because I didn't think hospitals were fashionable enough places for her to visit.

"Look at them," Cassie sneered as doctors strode past with purposeful steps, "their white coats are so bland and lacklustre. They need a makeover. I would perhaps add some accessories to make the white pop out. Maybe a nice black belt to give the coats definition and create a waist?"

I didn't reply because she wasn't really asking for my input.

Why had she come to see me?

The yearbook, of course.

I appreciated Cassie's lack of false modesty or pretention. She was blunt in the extreme, like a poker smashing down on a girl's head. Can you tell I'm still not over that yet?

TCR 01:52:49:26

"You need to get well soon," Cassie told me.

I smiled even though it hurt my face.

"Don't smile," Cassie shivered.

"Thank you for coming all the way here to see me," I whispered, my throat swollen and sore. Fluids were perpetually pumped through my body, delivered via a system of tubes, but despite all the nutrients that I needed to help me recover...I always felt thirsty.

"It wasn't any effort," Cassie said. "But we need you to write your tribute to Dan soon. After all, this accident has delayed my plans for the yearbook and I can't wait any longer."

Oh well, I thought.

The hospital had Wi-Fi, so I spent a few hours later that night watching

Cassie's vlog.

It was bizarre.

"If you want to stand out and be unique," Cassie declared in one broadcast, *"then you need to buy this cool new product called Ishara Mascara. However did I live without it? And it's so easy to use! You just take this special curved brush and apply it gently in a circular motion."*

A caption, so tiny it was almost unreadable, flashed up at the bottom of the screen:

I AM BEING PAID TO ADVERTISE THIS PRODUCT.

If my horrific first week at high school had taught me anything, it was that in order to *stand out* in the crowd, you had to *look like* the crowd. That was an epiphany. It took being smacked on the head with a heavy steel poker for me to realise the folly of my ways. Though my brain was bashed, I still thought about school and everything I'd been through. It hadn't been erased. Then, with a loud gasp, I realised in horror that…well…

…I'm Cassie Trendy's target audience.

If not for Dan, then I would probably be at the pharmacy buying Ishara Mascara.

In that lonely hospital room, I pined for Dan and the promise she'd offered. When I shut my eyes to sleep, I saw her dancing in the dark to the soundtrack of My Chemical Romance, as she joined in their black parade.

61

"Call Me Clive"

At first he appeared in my dreams, until it dawned on me that he was actually there in the room waiting for me to wake up. The last time we'd met, it was so he could ask me questions about Father and why he would have wanted to kill everyone during breakfast.

It was Inspector Guthrie.

You don't know this, Simon, but he visited me in hospital.

Oddly, he always seemed to me like the sort of man who would be a good dad.

Does that sound silly?

TCR 01:52:49:26

Inspector Guthrie – AKA "Call Me Clive" – is a decent and uncomplicated man who wants only to help people. During the events of The Final Prayer, in the midst of the chaos with those crime scene investigators and bodies of our Family, he took me aside and asked what I needed. That one small question made such a big difference. Father had never once asked me what I needed. I trusted Inspector Guthrie, but of course I couldn't tell him everything.

I want you to know that, Simon.

"I heard about your accident," Clive said as medical machines bleeped in the night.

Then his voice lowered into an accusing whisper:

"Are you ready to tell the truth?"

Yes, I'm ready to tell the truth – but Clive will have to wait his turn.

62

Return To The Sanctum

You'd spent hours decorating the house with nice banners for when I returned. I appreciated the gesture. Who wouldn't? It felt like a party had been thrown in my honour. But I don't have a good history with parties, so I didn't really feel like celebrating. WELCOME HOME STARRSHA, said one banner. WE LOVE YOU STARRSHA, said another, albeit in smaller letters. You took me in your arms and hugged me, but not too tight because you could tell my body was brittle. Then we walked together, arm-in-arm into the library, the second-largest room in the house.

I'm *so* glad you didn't take me into the study. I couldn't have handled it.

Imelda was in the library on the piano – not playing it, but sitting on the edge, swinging her legs absentmindedly. When she saw me she smiled, but it wasn't real.

None of it was real.

"Welcome back, Little Star!"

"Hello, Auntie," I said wearily. There was no point in fighting her, not yet. I didn't have the energy for another battle. Instead, I concentrated on my recovery.

"You've been through a terrible ordeal," Imelda told me in false sympathy, "and we wanted to cheer you up. It was Simon's idea to have this little party. I suggested we invite your friends at school but…"

Imelda covered her lips so you couldn't read them:

"It turns out you don't have any friends at school."

"Cassie Trendy is my best friend," I lied.

She laughed. And laughed. It wasn't *that* funny.

"Uncle Ezra must have rattled your skull with that poker," she said when you weren't looking, "because you really believe your lies."

Mention of Uncle Ezra's name made me remember what happened, as if I could have forgotten. It was always there whenever I looked in a mirror: the bruises that hadn't yet healed; the red puffy skin, the bandages wrapped around my head, my bulbous eyes...

TCR 01:54:10:28

"Where were you the day he attacked me?" I asked, dropping any attempt at civility.

"I was out shopping for shoes."

"I don't believe you!"

"Do you think I care what The Mummy thinks of me? Look at you! All bandaged up."

You were in the corner fixing one of the banners, the edge of which had slumped onto the carpet. You didn't see our lips making sentences. We were engaged in a fully-fledged argument. It was bound to happen, of course.

"When Uncle Ezra attacked me, I tried to escape but someone was holding the door from the other side. They left me there while he beat me."

Imelda's eyes narrowed and I could sense her fruitful mind thinking it over.

"I was out shopping for shoes," she repeated firmly.

Horribly enough...

I almost believed Auntie Imelda.

TCR 01:54:59:59

If it wasn't her and it wasn't you, then who was on the other side of that door when Ezra came for me? None of it made sense at the time. My insecurities and sore bones overwhelmed me, ensuring that my homecoming party was a horrible experience.

I couldn't enjoy myself knowing that someone out there had deliberately set me up.

But...who?

63

Sweet Valley High

As much as I tried to avoid Uncle Ezra, we had to live together and that meant planning my time carefully. The last thing I wanted to do was bump into him in the middle of the night. He'd probably bludgeon me with his Zimmer or something. I'd already decided to return to school, which would keep me out of The Sanctum for a good portion of the day. The rest of it could be spent in my bedroom reading my *Sweet Valley High* books. I love Jessica and Elizabeth. The adventures of the Wakefield sisters enthrall me. They're twin sisters, but constantly fight over petty things, even when getting into ridiculous situations. Jessica is a bad girl, constantly causing trouble. Elizabeth is the nice twin, bookish and withdrawn.

There are days I want to be Jessica…but I know I'll always be Elizabeth.

TCR 01:55:31:18

Reading those books helped pass the time while my bones healed. Don't dismiss the healing power of a good book. Books help you forget your problems.

But there was one problem that I couldn't forget, despite trying hard.

There was another videotape to watch.

It had been brought to The Sanctum by Uncle Ezra.

You wanted us to watch it together, which meant…

It meant being in the same room as him.

TCR 01:56:33:49

Once again we gathered in front of the old TV and VCR in The Secret Cinema and waited for someone to press <PLAY>. You sat between me and Uncle Ezra, who wittered to himself like a harmless old codger. Of course, he was anything *but* harmless. Anytime he shifted his weight on the chair, I moved mine away from him. If he even looked in my direction, I'd turn away and find myself face-to-face with Imelda, who also seemed very wary of being in a room with her older brother. Despite that, she'd brought a box of microwaveable popcorn, which she ate at a leisurely pace.

Imelda asked a very good question in the middle of eating:

"Why was the old Deacon so obsessed with videotapes?"

"We can't stream film up here," I explained, "the house is too deep in the woods to get a good signal. It isn't possible to have the internet let alone Netflix."

"Hmmm. Okay, so why didn't he just collect Blu-Rays or DVDs instead?"

"Father hated DVDs. They reminded him of Compact Discs."

"What's wrong with CDs?"

"Father preferred vinyl."

Imelda sighed wearily

"He was a pretentious old git, wasn't he?"

"A very *ostentatious* man," I added.

TCR 01:56:52:49

Finally, you stood up and raised the remote control in line with the television.

ARE WE ALL READY?

"Get on with it," Imelda moaned.

You got on with it.

The screen was awash with lines and flickering patterns until…

…Father appeared onscreen.

"Hello, Ezra," boomed his voice. *"You didn't expect to see me again, did you?"*

"We are all Sorak's children now," Uncle Ezra mumbled.

I shivered. The heating was on, so it wasn't cold that was making me feel so cold.

"I need you to do me a favour, Ezra. I'm gathering everyone together for a family reunion. I've even invited that little tramp Imelda."

She seethed as I laughed.

It was what she deserved for what she did during my homecoming party.

Father's voice lowered into a whisper, which you read easily, but we couldn't

135

hear. I lifted the remote control and turned the volume UP until his whisper was a static scream:

"I've been threatened, Ezra. The last few weeks I've been receiving some odd letters. They're stuffed under my bedroom door at night. They're left in the boxes of videos I'm going to watch. They're pinned up on the Prayer Board in the morning, waiting for me to find them. They're all signed Sorak The Almighty. This is clearly the work of a blasphemer. But who is it? I must root them out at once!"

Uncle Ezra stood up and yelled:

"It was Uncle Ezra in the study with the poker!"

"Sit down, you daft old loony," hissed Imelda, her hand scooping more popcorn.

"I'm trying to listen to the videotape!" I screamed.

They went quiet and we watched the rest of Father's message.

"If anything happens to me, then you will be in charge of my congregation. You will lead my Children in the ways of Sorak The Almighty. You will put them to work in the factory and ensure they meet all the deadlines for delivery. You'll find them a willing workforce as long as they realise they're doing it for a greater good…"

Father chuckled.

"I've made a lot of money from my disciples."

None of this seemed to surprise Imelda in the slightest.

"At least he admits the entire religion is nonsense!" she said.

"He did not," I shot back.

Father continued, completely unaware of the argument he'd started:

"My money is hidden away and it'll all go to you, Ezra."

Then Father uttered the words that would doom Uncle Ezra to a painful death:

"You'll soon be a millionaire."

64

Dead Man's Riddle

We looked at each other dumbly, wondering what would happen next. Father's message wasn't done. He was too much of a showman to end at that point. His face moved closer to the camera and seemed to push itself out from the TV screen.

"The money will help keep our little enterprise running. You can spend it all if you choose, but I know you, Ezra…I can always count on your greed…and it makes sense for you to take over The Church of Sorak The Almighty. Think of the fun you'll have with all those willing disciples. They'll do anything to please you in the name of Sorak."

Ezra chuckled gleefully and clapped his hands together.

TCR 01:57:47:28

Maybe it was good that The Family had perished during the Last Prayer. Please don't think badly of me for saying that, but the thought of Ezra having carte blanche to do what he wanted to everyone is too terrifying to contemplate.

TCR 01:57:59:59

Father continued his long boring eulogy. Not much had changed even in death.

"The turnover and profits from our oats over the last two years have been very handsome indeed, nearly as handsome as me. It helps that we're doing it for Sorak."

Father threw his head back and laughed hysterically, as though he alone knew the punchline to a terrible joke. Then he sobered up and addressed us sombrely.

"If I am indeed dead, then you must ensure the disciples don't play up. They might try to demand money for their work. Some are in this country illegally. Use

that to threaten them. I do. It always works. Simon is a bit difficult. He pretends he can't understand you if he doesn't want to do something, but don't underestimate that lad. He may be deaf, but he certainly isn't dumb."

Your face darkened, as did my mood.

"My three wives are all useless," Father said sadly. *"They're boring. But you might find Dorinda a good diversion if you can keep Linden away from her. I promised him he could have her if he ruled this place wisely in my absence. But he's a fool. And that's why you sit here today, a millionaire and the new Deacon of Glowglass."*

At first I thought he wouldn't mention me.

Until he did:

"As for Starrsha…"

"Oh no," I cried out.

"My Little Star will continue to serve in the Church. She'll use my death as an opportunity to attend some wretched school. Pull her out at once. Education is an experiment that failed. She became untrustworthy and treacherous."

"What!"

Uncle Ezra covered his ears and hissed something about 'evil', which made me tense up for a fight. I didn't want him to give me another unwanted facelift with a poker. It still hurt to smile, which wasn't a big problem as I barely had any reason to these days.

Please don't think I'm feeling sorry for myself. It's just a fact.

"I'm going back to school," I declared firmly.

You nodded in agreement.

"But it's The Deacon's final wish that Starrsha not go to school."

Imelda. She couldn't help kicking me while I was down. I suppose it was easier to kick someone while wearing an expensive pair of Louboutin heels.

Father departed with a final thought:

"I have so much waiting for you, Ezra. Please take charge and rule with all the might you can muster. If whoever wrote those letters does make good on his promise to get me, then you must ensure they suffer. Hurt them, Ezra. Hurt them for me!"

"He's vile," Imelda muttered.

At least we agreed on something.

"If you want to find the money, go to the place where there are no men allowed.

You'll know what I mean, Ezra. I've made sure you and you alone will get the key."

The message stopped abruptly.

We watched helplessly as the picture on the TV screen froze.

Father's nasty smile crackled with static.

"Get it off the screen," I shrieked.

The ringing in my ears was loud and painful.

No-one moved.

I leapt up from my chair and rushed over to the VCR, where I jabbed the <EJECT> button frantically. The video cassette spat out the front of the machine. I grabbed it and chucked it at the wall with all the strength I could summon.

His smile was gone.

That was all that mattered.

TCR 01:58:27:10

65

Paint, Patience And Hair Dye

The Yearbook was cancelled after it emerged that Cassie Trendy had stolen the money she'd raised in order to pay off an enormous credit card bill. Her scheme was uncovered when one of the fourth-year students – a girl known to everyone as The Weave Queen – discovered that Cassie had used Dan's death as a way of raising extra money to fund her impossibly glamourous lifestyle. The Weave Queen – real name Chrissie Gunderson – had a YouTube vlog that was a rival of Cassie's. Something had had to give in the war between Cassie and Chrissie, and that something was The Yearbook.

So, there you have it. The real reason Cassie became my friend. She needed me to convince people to fund the yearbook, which in turn would fund her shopping sprees. Dan's death had served her well over the last few weeks. Isn't that disgusting?

TCR 01:59:42:27

"It's a lie," Cassie hissed at me one day while we were in the canteen at lunchtime, "and they can't prove I took that money."

The reason she was hissing at *me* in the canteen was because no-one else would sit with her. Cassie was officially the second most unpopular girl at Morvern High – after me, of course. What could I say to her? My thoughts lay elsewhere, in a place between porridge and mass murder. Father's money weighed heavily in my imagination. He had summoned Imelda and Ezra back to cause trouble, tempting them with riches beyond their wildest imagination. And now they were searching for his fortune and...I was at Morvern High listening to Cassie go on about her own financial problems.

Cassie was lying to me and I couldn't stand her insincerity a second longer. As Sorak The Almighty once said:

Patience is like a bottle of hair dye. It eventually runs out.

We spent our lunch in silence, which suited me fine because I wanted to figure out the answer to Father's strange riddle. I thought back to his video message for Uncle Ezra:

"If you want to find the money, go to the place where there are no men allowed."

Ezra was meant to understand what Father meant, but Uncle was so senile that he had forgotten the answer to the odd riddle. My thoughts were elsewhere, but my eyes remained fixed on Cassie as she idly picked at her lunch. Whatever did her penne pasta do to her? She thrust at the poor pasta tubes with her fork until they were skewered into submission, then she shoved a load into her mouth, chewing until they were no more.

Once done, she repeated the process until the plate was clear.

It was a penne pasta massacre.

"What?" Cassie asked, whilst wiping her lips with a napkin.

"I didn't say anything," I said.

"Yes, you did."

"What did I say?"

"Something about 'the place where there are no men allowed', I think."

TCR 02:00:00:00

My high school reputation as a freak was bad enough, but being seen talking to myself was probably the next logical step in ruining my status beyond repair. Cassie, however, didn't seem to care about my little quirks. She was the centre of her universe and only one matter occupied her thoughts: Herself.

Restoring her prestige was Cassie's top priority. I knew she'd find a way to get back to the top of the social ladder, kicking everyone down as she climbed over them.

In that context, she didn't care that I was muttering to myself during lunch.

TCR 02:00:44:19

"It's a riddle," I explained, "something I've got to answer for a project."

Obviously I didn't tell her that the riddle would make me a teenage millionaire.

"If I knew a place men weren't allowed, I'd move there today."

"It's a weird one," I agreed.

"How about a bench?"

"Huh?"

"A memorial bench. If we can't have a yearbook then I could try and get everyone interested in a memorial bench dedicated to Dan."

She wasn't listening to me. My riddle was vital. It had to be answered as soon as possible before Imelda and Uncle Ezra solved it and uncovered the money.

Then Cassie surprised me by saying, "A memorial bench will get everyone onside." Her words were accompanied by a flick of her fake hair.

A sudden urge to slap the make-up right off her face overwhelmed me, but I successfully cast it aside. Again she was using my friend to rebuild her reputation at Morvern High. Why was she so interested in any memorial for Dan? She didn't know or care about Dan. She'd shown no interest in her while she was alive, so this sudden streak of benevolence didn't fool me. It wasn't about Dan.

It was about Cassie.

Cassie is so wonderful!

Cassie is so thoughtful!

Cassie is…fake.

I wanted to puke my lunch across the table; to binge and purge the way I had for years.

Instead I smiled and agreed it was a good idea.

Honestly, it wasn't like it would ever happen. She'd been accused of ripping off the entire school for her aborted yearbook. But here's the lesson to be learned: not only did she get permission to have a memorial bench built in the centre of the schoolyard, but she did it with monstrous efficiency.

The bench was unveiled ten days after we first had the conversation in the school canteen. The day after we all gathered to witness its inauguration, the bench was vandalised.

Something was splattered on it.

Can you guess what?

DYKE, of course.

66

Revenge Without Porridge

It *had* to be Rhona.

My mind flashed back to that day in the changing rooms when Rhona had terrorised Dan with that one word. I told you about it earlier. Dan's sexuality was an obsession with that girl. She lured me and my best friend to her damn party and then everything crumbled around me. My new life was under siege and I'd finally had enough.

I'm not proud, Simon, but I had to do it.

I had to take revenge on them all. They had to pay for their crimes against Dan.

Sorak The Almighty would have approved, after all he once proclaimed:

An eye for an eye, a tooth for a tooth, and worst of all…a leak in their roof.

The next few nights were spent in my bedroom, thinking up plans to avenge myself against Rhona and Aimee. Oh yes, she had to suffer too. Aimee had gotten away with too much thanks to her charm. When she denied having anything to do with Dan, everyone automatically believed her, which meant they all looked at Dan as a liar.

Poor Dan.

I want to listen to My Chemical Romance albums in tribute to her but…

But I need to finish my story.

I've been speaking for over two hours.

I don't know how long this videotape will last.

You need to let me finish this once and for all, Simon.

TCR 02:02:10:51

My scheme took me away from the important matter of the riddle. My hope was that if I stopped thinking about it, the answer would blossom in my brain. Imelda would sneak past my bedroom door and listen in hope of hearing me talk to myself. Blabbing to people is quite a bad habit of mine. But I would keep this all to myself. I'd learned from that lunch hour with Cassie Trendy not to be so careless.

You kept away from me too.

It seemed like a lifetime ago that we were the only ones here in The Sanctum. I miss those days.

67

Sasha Jenkins

While she was alive, Dan warned me to stay away from Sasha Jenkins. She was, in Dan's words, "a nutty nutter," which meant nothing to me as a girl who'd survived mass murder. She didn't give a reason but I knew she was right. Sasha looked like a wrestler. A CROCODILE wrestler. Honestly, one of those big meaty hands could inflict damage.

I should know. I saw it with my own eyes.

TCR 02:03:17:51

It happened one day on the way to Computing Science.

I'd stopped by my locker to get some books when something shot past me.

There was a disturbance in the air, a slight rippling effect.

Whatever had barrelled past was fast and powerful.

"What…?" I asked myself in bewilderment.

That's when Sasha made it clear that she was here to fight.

She was angry with someone, a girl from third year that I didn't know.

"You want him!" Sasha screamed hoarsely, the sound of someone who shouted so much that she'd worn-out her poor tonsils. There are special honeyed teas that could help her with that problem, I thought at the time. But I didn't say that aloud.

Instead I waited – and watched.

"I wouldn't even touch that with a cattle prod," the girl at the locker yelled back, but her voice was smaller. She shrivelled under the towering force of Sasha's height. Suddenly the corridor seemed to freeze so that everyone could watch. The situation could go two ways: it could smoulder until it stopped, or ignite suddenly into a fiery fight.

This is high school.

We teenagers are ticking time bombs of hormones.

I know I am.

Someone yelled 'FIGHT!' and Sasha made her decision.

She punched the girl right into her locker with enough force to rattle the entire row.

I squealed.

Others cheered.

The prefects arrived to put a stop to the fight...

"Stop making an article of yourself," the Head Prefect said in a shrill voice.

Sasha punched her too.

TCR 02:04:01:37

None of this led to Sasha being expelled, though she really should have been. But I'm so glad she wasn't. She proved very useful to me in my secret war against Rhona and Aimee. Very useful indeed. I have to believe there was a special reason why the headmaster kept Sasha at Morvern High when he could have hurled her out of the school gates forever. It was like someone wanted me to win.

Praise Sorak The Almighty!

68

(How I Caused A) Teenage Punching Spree

Approaching Sasha was like dipping your forearm into a bucket of blood and thrusting it under the nose of Dracula. I had to be careful because I didn't want to be her next victim.

She was at her favourite place in Morvern High. Where? The front of the queue in the canteen at lunchtime.

She undertook this ritual on a daily basis: the bell would trill and she'd walk into the canteen, heading past everyone to the front, regardless of how long the others had waited. Nobody dared question her or say anything aloud. They valued their bones too much to have them broken.

It was with trepidation that I entered the canteen. There was always a danger that Cassie Trendy might grab me to help her with the lunchtime poll, a useless feature of the school newspaper. Instead, I walked confidently past everybody until I was at the very front with Sasha Jenkins.

Sasha, however, seemed pleased to see me. She gave me the same expression that she usually reserved for cheeseburgers and chips. Two girls muttered behind me, but that's all they did. Sasha looked around and started up a conversation, just as I'd hoped.

Her opening comment, however, took me completely by surprise.

"I wish I could be like you," she said chirpily.

"Me? Why?"

"I heard you were home-schooled before you came to Morvern High."

"Oh," I said, immediately brightening at the memories of Miss Gibson, my beloved tutor. "Well it was certainly different, but I enjoyed it. I like being here too."

"I'd like to be home-schooled," Sasha admitted with a voice on the wistful side of sad.

"Don't you like Morvern High?"

"Nah. Everyone makes fun of me and I get so mad. But I'm working on it. I have an anger management councillor."

"Most teenagers have acne. You have an anger management councillor."

"People make fun of you too," Sasha said, though I already knew. "They laugh at your clothes and all the really long words you use. They think you're trying too hard."

"I think I need the number of your anger management councillor."

Sasha laughed at that one. Which made what I was about to do even more disgraceful.

But then I thought of Dan's bench and the word scrawled on it.

Suddenly I felt less unpleasant about my plan.

"I wanted to speak to you but…"

It wasn't an accident that I let my sentence trail away into silence. I'd practiced.

"But?" Sasha asked, her interest suddenly piqued.

"I don't know if I can tell you," I said, looking furtively around the canteen.

I'd rehearsed this particular facial expression in the mirror until I looked suitably shifty.

"Tell me what?"

This was a dangerous thing I was about to do.

Sasha's voice hardened at the same time as her fists clenched.

I thought of the party and Dan in a coffin with her hair styled the wrong way.

"If I tell you, will you promise never to say anything to anyone?"

"Is someone talking about me behind my back? Are they saying stuff that's untrue? Are they after Kenneth? If someone's trying to steal my Kenneth you'd better tell me!"

TCR 02:04:48:59

Kenneth Keenan is her weakness. He's the person Sasha loves above all else in the entire world. They'd walk down the corridors of Morvern together, hands held tightly, a shield against the rumours and laughter. While she was a giant, he was small; very small. According to Dan, the school had set up a fundraising day on Kenneth's behalf. "They tried to do something good," she told me, "so we all had to take part in a carnival right here in the schoolyard." The aim was to raise money to pay for an operation that would stretch Kenny until he was 'average' height.

Unfortunately for Kenny, the school didn't raise enough funds.

There's something tragic about a failed fundraiser.

Sasha didn't care. She loved Kenny ardently.

And yet…

If Dan was to be believed – and I believed her completely – their relationship would never work out in the end.

Why?

Sasha isn't Kenny's type *at all*.

TCR 02:05:25:41

"Nobody is trying to steal Kenny," I told her, trying my hardest to soothe Sasha before she beat up the entire lunch queue. But that didn't mean I wanted her tamed completely.

"I'm ready to eat my cheeseburger and fries," Sasha growled, "but before I do that, you need to tell me what's going on and what you're keeping from me!"

"Dan's charity bench."

"What about it?"

"I heard someone sprayed the word *dyke* on it about you."

"What?" Sasha screamed.

The lady behind the counter dumped a cheeseburger and a serving of fries onto Sasha's tray. She seemed eager to get rid of her and start the queue flowing forward.

"I've got a man and he loves me. Who did it? Tell me the names of the jealous bitches! Who called me a dyke?" Sasha asked between gritted teeth. Her eyes were wide and bloodshot, as though corpuscles had filled up too fast and burst under the pressure of Sasha's boiling reaction. Her face quickly turned a shade of pinky blue.

"Rhona and Aimee both think Kenny is your cover story," I explained.

Sasha lifted her cheeseburger and tore into it with a feral bite.

I liked to imagine it was a practice run for what she intended to do to my enemies.

TCR 02:06:59:58

69

Cracking The Clue

You came to my room later that night to see me, a gesture I appreciated. You hadn't come by for a while and I missed you a lot. It had become lonely living in a house full of people. In all honesty, it was like being at school. Sometimes I'd get hungry because I didn't want to eat dinner with Imelda and Mad Uncle Ezra, so I resorted to sneaking around at night, raiding the cupboards for food. This meant I was in a position to see Imelda and Crazy Uncle Ezra doing the same thing; only *they* weren't looking for food. They never once realised I was hiding behind couches, around corners or inside empty rooms. It always amazes me how big The Sanctum is and how many rooms are in this place – rooms with locked doors I'd never crossed. But then Imelda was doing more than enough 'exploring' for all of us; she was on the hunt for something to help solve Father's odd riddle. They had no idea where to look or how to resolve it.

TCR 02:07:38:10

"Thank you for coming to see me," I said, reclining on my bed with a book.

It wasn't a *Sweet Valley High* novel, for once. It was a book I had to read for English, a paperback edition of *Jane Eyre*, a ridiculous story about a governess trapped in an abusive relationship with her employer. He's determined to make her his mistress and she seems up for it. After his fiancé spurns his advances and his wife dies suspiciously after being locked up for years (no wonder she went crazy) he finally marries Jane and they live together, despite his attempted bigamy.

Good luck with that one, Jane Eyrehead.

You were dressed in a red flannel shirt with a pair of blue denim jeans. They were new. Goodness, I thought, when did you go shopping? That made me realise how far we'd drifted apart. There was a time when we'd have gone together into town just like we used to in the weeks after Father and The Family went to Heaven.

HAVE YOU SOLVED THE RIDDLE YET?

"No."

I THOUGHT YOU WOULD HAVE ANSWERED IT BY NOW.

"I've been busy with other things at school."

There was an uneasy silence between the two of us.

IMELDA IS STILL TRYING. EZRA JUST POTTERS ABOUT ALONE.

"If Sorak The Almighty wishes it, then they'll find the answer."

You frowned slightly, and I read your face as easily as the frayed edition of Jane Eyre in my hands: you didn't believe me. You thought I'd solved the riddle but for some reason didn't want to tell you I'd already cracked it.

You were right, actually.

I'd succeeded in unravelling Father's stupid riddle.

Do you want to know how?

I'm going to explain it, but don't bother going to check.

I've already got the key.

It's for a safety deposit box in a vault at the bank in town.

But that box will never be opened.

Sorry about that.

70
The Women (1939)

How did I solve the riddle and find the key to the safety deposit box?

An old memory dislodged in my brain, once again hurling me back into the past. There was something in his words – the way he had spoken when he had announced his riddle to Crazy Uncle Ezra – that had stayed with me in the following weeks:

"If you want to find the money, go to the place where there are no men allowed."

It didn't take me long to figure out that it was a movie reference of some sort.

One night, whilst sneaking downstairs for food...I found myself creeping into The Secret Cinema to hide from Uncle Ezra as he clomped down the hallway towards the toilet. I hid in the corner beneath a tower of video tapes, praying I'd remain hidden, breathing so slightly that my head felt like it might burst.

Then my eyes fell upon a particular videotape.

One of Father's old movies.

And I recalled the day the postman had delivered a dead woman's false eyelashes to Father.

TCR 02:08:18:58

"Do you know what these are?" he said to me.

They looked like the plucked legs of a spider, but I didn't say anything. The last thing I wanted to do was look foolish in front of The Deacon.

"They're Joan Crawford's eyelashes!" Father yelled, his excitement making him loud.

He looked utterly stupid. There he stood, a grown man dressed in an expensive bespoke two-piece suit from some fancy tailor, getting all hot and bothered over a set of fake eyelashes that…some actress with terrible shoulder pads had worn years ago.

"Joan Crawford was a powerful lady," he explained, "a great actress. No, to call her an *actress* does her an injustice. She was a star!"

It made absolutely no difference to me.

"Her best movie was *Mildred Pierce*," he continued, oblivious to the fact that all I wanted was for Miss Gibson to arrive with my books, so we could study and I could learn. But Father was more interested in quoting Joan Crawford's filmography.

"*The Women* is another masterpiece."

"*The Women*?" I asked without any interest.

"It's a movie from 1939 and not a single man appears in it. The entire cast is women. Even the animals in it are female."

I put this out of my mind, but it waited for the right moment to pop up again.

TCR 02:10:19:27

Years later, when I found myself hiding in The Secret Cinema, terrified that Uncle Ezra would burst my skull like a ripe watermelon for a second time, the memory of Father and the fake eyelashes suddenly played out before me, my eyes a substitute screen – their own secret cinema. It didn't take me long to find a box labelled *THE WOMEN (1939)*. My hands cautiously reached out for it, trembling at the thought of knocking over the towering pile of video cassettes and alerting Ezra and Imelda, but I remained quiet despite my excitement.

"If you want to find the money, go to the place where there are no men allowed."

I opened the videotape edition of *The Women* – a movie without a single man in it – and cautiously tipped the cassette out of the box to find…

A single key stuck to the surface of the black plastic by a single piece of tape.

There was another surprise awaiting me.

Sitting behind the pile of old videotapes was a large cardboard box. My interest caught, I blew the layer of dust off it, creating a dust whirlwind in the process. The earthy smell of damp made me gag slightly, but I battled through it and looked inside.

I'd discovered an old camcorder.

I'm using it right now, to record my message to you.

Hello!

TCR 02:12:04:07

71

A Reversed Charge
Phone Call From Heaven

Everything was going well in my life.

Almost everything.

Sasha still hadn't sorted out Rhona and Aimee, who had escaped without a single blemish to their reputations despite Dan's death. They were free and walking around Morvern High without a care or worry. Do you know what kept me sane? It was the thought that in my left trouser pocket was a key that would unlock a brand-new life for us. Whatever Father had promised Uncle Ezra would instead go to us, the two people who had suffered most under his reign of terror. We'd get our inheritance and so much more besides!

Even Sorak The Almighty was happy for me.

I know because He phoned me one day while I was on the bus.

TCR 02:12:48:51

It was a school trip to see a production of *Romeo & Juliet* at the local theatre. I was the only person on the bus sitting by myself, as no-one wanted to be seen with me. Cassie Trendy, my sort-of-friend, rushed by and pretended not to notice me when I waved.

The bus was halfway through an intersection when my mobile phone buzzed angrily.

"Hello," a pleasant voice said from the phone, *"we have a caller here who would like to reverse the charges. It's a Mr..."* The voice halted as though the owner of it couldn't quite make out the name in front of her. Eventually, she decided to just say it aloud:

"Sorak Almighty."

"What's a reversed charges call?" I asked.

"You pay for the caller's phone call," the woman said lightly.

It made sense to me; after all, why would Sorak The Almighty carry money? He clearly had no problem with his followers *making* money, but He wasn't keen on material wealth for Himself. Some might find that hypocritical, but it's just life, isn't it?

"Okay," I said after a long pause, "put Him through."

The bus, until then alive with noise, fell very quiet as my classmates watched and listened to the one-way conversation between me and a holy spirit.

"Where is the key?" Sorak hissed.

"The key?" I asked innocently.

"The key my disciple left behind on this lowly realm."

"The key is safe," I said.

"Safe where?"

"The safe is in the bank," I responded wickedly.

"What?"

"The key is safe and the safe is in the bank."

"I want you to place the key on the church alter tonight," commanded the voice.

I decided to put a question to my deity:

"What do you think about liars?"

"Liars will drown in a pool of eternal damnation."

"Okay. What did you say in Volume Three of your *Black Books* about liars?"

Sorak The Almighty, the most powerful of cosmic forces in creation, choked.

"I command you to leave the key on my holy altar!"

"So you can collect it later? No, I don't think so. Why would you need a key anyway? You're omnipotent. Surely you could just *open* the safety deposit box?"

158

The bus driver pulled a face that I caught in the surface of the window.

They all think I'm insane.

That's my reputation.

Let them think it. I know who I am and what I've done.

"You are not Sorak The Almighty," I said with a sigh.

The caller laughed. Actually laughed. It was a throaty cackle that grated my eardrums.

"Have a nice day," I told the caller as I pressed the red button to kill the conversation.

Incidentally, here's what Sorak *actually* has to say about liars:

A liar is about as reliable as a flat tyre.

TCR 02:14:18:37

72

Escalators

Romeo & Juliet was really good. Well...the part I was allowed to see, at least. I was halfway through watching it when one of the teachers suddenly remembered there was a suicide pact at the very end. Unfortunately, I'd become the poster girl for suicide after what happened at The Sanctum during The Final Prayer. Juliet only used poison – not poison and porridge – to kill herself. The teachers, however, felt it would be 'truly insensitive' to subject me to an onstage recreation of suicide.

My protests fell on unforgiving ears:

"We need to get her out of here," Mr Martens said, his face red and bloated from all the strenuous activity he was doing on my behalf. I was dragged from the audience and into the hallway of the old theatre, the carpets of which were similar in colour to my teacher's ruddy big face. Rich hues of red should have made the place feel expensive; instead, the theatre seemed a bit lost and faded.

"I want to see the end of the play," I begged.

A few minutes later I found myself sitting alone on the bus. Mr Martens apologised and informed me that he'd be back soon. He probably wanted to see the end of the play himself, a pleasure he was denying me.

"Life sucks," I said aloud.

The minutes dragged slowly by and I played a few songs from my DAN'S FAVOURITE SONGS playlist on my iPhone. It wasn't ideal, but I enjoyed the peace and quiet. My hands shook with hunger and reminded me that I hadn't eaten breakfast. I don't do breakfast anymore. You understand, I know. But I decided to leave the bus and head back into the theatre to get myself a snack, to quieten my angry belly. Obey the belly, that's what I say. I've treated it badly in the past.

TCR 02:15:15:49

The foyer was empty bar a few people behind various counters. Each person regarded me with an expression of annoyance, as though I'd interrupted their precious private time. The fact that they were being paid to serve me didn't seem to matter.

"I'd like some popcorn," I whispered, thinking of Imelda.

"Wrong place," the woman behind the counter laughed.

I'd mixed up the theatre with the cinema.

"You can have some chocolate peanuts if you want," the woman added, thrusting a bag into my hands.

"Thank you," I said, receiving the food gratefully.

Money changed hands and I headed back to the bus to gorge on the bag of chocolate peanuts. It was while I was sitting there eating that the play ended. The doors swung open and hordes of people burst through, moving towards the downward escalator.

Remember I said earlier that a set of escalators would be significant in my story?

TA-DAH!

I watched the commotion with my face pressed against the glass, smudges of me on the surface. I couldn't hear much from inside the bus, but I definitely heard the scream.

It was quick and sounded like someone in real pain.

Not that I'm a connoisseur of screams, but I've got experience, haven't I?

"What happened?" I yelled from the bus.

Cassie Trendy bounded over from the crowd that was encircling the bottom of the escalator. Her face was flushed with excitement. I'd seen a similar expression in one of her videos advertising a new version of Ishara Mascara.

"It's Aimee," she panted from outside the bus. "She fell down the escalator."

I lifted my bag of chocolate peanuts and tossed one into my mouth.

The chocolate melted and tasted extra yummy.

"Praise Sorak," I said with a gooey smile.

161

73

White Heat

Aimee lay slumped at the bottom of the escalator, her hair matted with blood. She'd taken quite a tumble down the moving stairs and had fallen hard against the furrowed metal surface. Worse, her hair had been caught between stairs, leading some plucky classmate to hit the Emergency Stop switch. He probably saved her life.

The Princess Di of Morvern High screamed as someone called for an ambulance.

I looked around, my eyes darting to and fro, hoping to find someone in particular.

Sasha was nearby, sipping from a straw on a cup of Coca-Cola.

"Did you do that?"

She seemed surprised by my question. Her eyes blinked twice, lazy and slow.

When she finally spoke, it was with a mocking tone.

"Nah. The silly cow tripped and fell."

The trauma was too much for some of my classmates. They wept openly for their fallen princess as she lay still on the ground, waiting not for a prince but a paramedic to whisk her off to hospital. She lay at an odd angle, twisted and unnatural. The theatre had been closed to the public temporarily, which meant nobody was getting in…or leaving.

"Well done," I whispered.

Sasha Jenkins slurped the dregs of her drink and said:

"She'll think twice before calling me a dyke again."

That's all she said on the matter, never once admitting or denying what she'd done to Aimee. It was a form of justice, delivered in a different way. Aimee had been in some sort of secret relationship with Dan and her denial at Rhona's party had started a chain of events that had led to my best friend freezing to death alone in the night.

A part of me felt bad for Aimee, but it was a very small part and easily ignored.

TCR 02:17:04:11

The ambulance arrived a few minutes later, dramatically cutting through the traffic outside the theatre, with blaring horns and spinning lights. We all crowded around the door, waiting for the medics to come through and save Aimee, whose sodden hair lay in a puddle of blood.

The medics, however, weren't alone.

A police car pulled up beside the ambulance.

My insides churned with fear as policemen approached the sealed doors.

I recognised one of them from the day our Family died, when The Sanctum was full to bursting with policemen and forensic detectives.

The policeman standing a few feet away from me at the theatre was the same man who took you away for questioning on The Day of the Final Prayer. We were in The Sanctum, waiting for the bodies to be taken away. I didn't expect you to go too.

"We need to ask Simon a few questions," the policeman said as you were led away in handcuffs.

My reply?

"Will you tell me what Simon says?"

I always found that totally hilarious.

TCR 02:17:54:56

There he was again in front of me with his uniform and furrowed brow.

A ghost from the past.

A premonition of the future?

74

The Return Of Call Me Clive

What started off as revenge against Aimee and Rhona quickly fell out of control. I'd started something and it was too late to stop. I'm so scared, Simon. I've been scared since The Day of the Final Prayer. Every single day I'm frightened. Do you know what it's like to constantly be afraid? It's heavy, like carrying a backpack full of bricks; an invisible backpack with invisible bricks. I can't breathe. I...oh I can't breathe...

I CAN'T BREATHE.

Huff huff huff...breathe girl...it's just a panic attack...breathe slowly... *huff...huff...*

The timer on the camcorder screen is counting everything away.

It won't be long.

I have to finish.

TCR 02:21:00:00

I feel like Father has reached into my brain and clenched his fist.

He's there, in me, trying to make me into him.

And you?

You're your Father's son, even if you aren't his *actual* son.

TCR 02:21:29:50

The day Aimee fell down the escalators of the Theatre Royal was the moment it started to go wrong for me. Yes, I know *lots* of things have gone wrong for me. I'm not called The Oatmeal Girl for nothing. But I was on top of the situation. I was in control. Now I'm a victim again. And it was rotten bad luck that ruined everything.

As Sorak The Almighty said in his *Iconic Books*:

Sorak The Almighty didn't invent the concept of Karma, but he likes it enough to pretend He did.

When those police officers looked over in my direction, their eyes homed in on my face, as if I was in an ID line-up at their station. They recognised me. Worse, they remembered me. How could they not? I knew things wouldn't remain the same for long.

To be honest, I don't know exactly what happened. But one of the policemen must have gone back to the station, filed his report and alerted one of his friends. Maybe they looked at the case files again, or perhaps my recent stint in hospital made them suspicious that things weren't quite...right. Whatever. The consequences of my carelessness – and bad luck – meant I'd drawn too much attention to myself.

That's why Inspector Guthrie, AKA Call Me Clive, came to the house.

Just in time for everyone to discover the dead body.

75

Kill Uncle

We were gathered by the main door of The Sanctum, the bleak mood between us the only thing we had in common by then. At this point you and the others had no idea I'd cracked Father's riddle. Yes, even as you stood beside me waiting for Guthrie to reach us, you didn't know there was a little key in my left trouser pocket.

And I had no idea what the key would bring me.

Something good, I hoped.

We were at the door in the hall because a police car was driving up the crumbling old road towards The Sanctum. Imelda guessed we were about to receive some company. We arrived one at a time until all three of us stood waiting expectantly.

A few moments later there was a heavy policeman's knock at the door.

The sound of knuckles against wood was almost as loud as the Avon saleswoman who braved the Glowglass Estate from time to time in order to sell us eternal youth and lies.

Imelda opened the door.

She was wearing…well, for her it was quite conservative…two belts over her chest and a pair of hot pants and heels. Poor Inspector Guthrie didn't know where to look. I almost suggested he look at the framed portrait of Father hanging in the hallway. I'd defaced the painting during a night-time sojourn, adding some horns. No-one had noticed, and I was slightly annoyed.

"Hello," Imelda said breathily, all fake and affected.

Guthrie didn't know Imelda. She hadn't been here when everyone died.

"Hey, Inspector," I offered.

"Call me Clive," he replied in a smooth voice.

"Why are you here?" I asked.

He looked right at me but remained silent.

The few seconds that he didn't speak felt like hours, until…

"I'd like to ask a few questions about what happened at the Theatre Royal."

SHE WAS AWAY ON A TRIP WITH HER SCHOOL, you said with fluctuating fingers. Imelda repeated your words aloud so Call Me Clive understood.

"I'm aware of that," he nodded, "but I'm following up on a few leads."

"Leads?" Imelda smiled.

I really wanted to tell Sasha Jenkins that Imelda was trying to steal her Kenny, just so I could watch Imelda get punched out of existence. But that wouldn't work again.

Suddenly, incidentally, I realised Uncle Ezra wasn't in the hall with us.

I thought nothing of it at the time.

Stupid, eh?

TCR 02:22:42:39

"I questioned Aimee Curtis at the hospital. You were at hospital recently, weren't you Starrsha?"

"Yes," I said, touched at Inspector Guthrie's concern for my welfare.

"What happened to Starrsha's classmate?" Imelda asked.

She knew what had happened. Well, she knew what I'd told you a few days earlier while she was in the same room. The only reason I'd told you was because I *knew* the police would get involved at some point. Barring amnesia – and I'm not that lucky – Aimee would explain what had happened.

My name was bound to come up at some point.

"She had an accident," Guthrie explained, completely unaware that Imelda already knew and was just trying to mess me around.

"Why are you here?" I blurted out.

Ah. That was careless, wasn't it?

"I wanted to speak to Starrsha about all the incidents that have taken place around her over the last few months."

"I want my lawyer."

"He's too busy helping old Deacon Glowglass from beyond the grave," Imelda cackled.

Guthrie, or Call Me Clive, spoke again, this time with his policeman voice, which was different to his nice normal way of speaking. It sounded condemning, even a little harsh.

"Do you *need* a lawyer?"

Yes, I did. But if I said so I'd look guilty.

If I said no, then I could fall into a trap.

There was only one response that I could give Detective Guthrie:

"No," I mumbled, finally.

"Okay," Call Me Clive said, whilst flicking through a small notepad.

WHERE IS UNCLE EZRA? you asked.

Call Me Clive didn't see your fingers making words into a question.

I shrugged.

"Aimee Curtis told two of my officers that she didn't trip – that she was pushed. In her statement she said, quote, *'I felt a hand on my back and the hand shoved me.'*"

"You can't take what she said seriously," I cried out.

Then I panicked.

Not like me at all.

"It was Sasha Jenkins."

Call Me Clive frowned.

He opened his mouth to speak when…

Another noise blotted out his voice.

It was the scream of an old man plunging to his death.

TCR 02:24:00:49

76

Pensioner Death Plunge

We found Mad Uncle Ezra at the bottom of the stairwell that led down into the guts of The Sanctum. It was the same staircase that we descended on the way to The Secret Cinema, the same wing of the house with the locked red door.

All of us made the morbid discovery at the same time.

The little body was warped into a weird angle, just like Aimee's when she'd fallen.

Just like Aimee's.

That was all I could think... Just like Aimee's.

TCR 02:24:31:15

Inspector Guthrie had arrived after being tipped off about one of my classmates falling down a moving staircase, only to find Uncle Ezra – the same dear old man who put me in hospital – at the bottom of a staircase in similar circumstances.

It was almost as if someone wanted me to look as bad as possible.

I was at both locations, I was the common link, and so it had to be my fault, right?

Wrong. I was with Inspector Guthrie when Uncle Ezra fell down the stairs. Thank goodness!

"Poor Uncle Ezra," I said, trying to sound sympathetic. "What a terrible accident."

"Just like that poor girl who fell down the theatre's escalator," Imelda added.

I looked at her with loathing. She reflected my look right back at me.

The little key in my left trouser pocket suddenly felt heavier.

77

Step On Me

We had to wait patiently while Uncle Ezra's corpse was removed from Glowglass Estate in a body bag. It was a familiar scene, the second time it had played out in under a year. Grim, but true. And as we all waited in the kitchen, with two policemen by the back door, I found my gaze moving towards Imelda, probing her reaction.

It had to be her, because I knew it couldn't be you. How did she manage it? She had to have figured out a way to make Ezra fall, and then got rid of the evidence while we weren't looking. She was crafty and brilliant, in her own way.

TCR 02:25:13:49

"Isn't it weird how people die in suspicious circumstances when they're around you?"

I didn't reply. Imelda was trying to test me. You didn't see because she made sure her lips were covered when she insulted me. She was good at being evil. She certainly wasn't good at anything else, unless you count bad fashion as talent.

"The police will probably want to re-open the files and look at your friend's death again. What was her name? Danny or something?"

She's right, you know. The police will take a closer look at my life.

They'll no doubt find that certain parts of it make no sense.

And that's why I've got to tell you the truth.

Let's go back to...

78

The Day Of The Final Prayer

It was a morning like any other due to the stifling heat and monotonous routine. The oat processing plant fell quiet for a short time while we all prepared ourselves for the morning sermon. There was plenty of work to be done, which meant this would be a short prayer service. I went about my usual schedule, which meant I had to get ready and help in the kitchen. Yet there I lay, in bed, trying to move…only to find I couldn't.

I was so hungry.

My hands trembled and my legs felt dead.

All I could think of was food.

Cake, chocolate, crisps, biscuits.

Anything but a bowl of salty stodgy porridge.

Perhaps I could hold off until lunch?

Being hungry wasn't so bad, I told myself, because it reminded me I was alive.

How stupid was I?

Sister Dorinda noticed how weak I looked as we headed into the kitchen to soak the oats for breakfast. Lovely, wonderful, fiery Sister Dorinda, forever fighting, continually losing. But the very fact that she fought back against her oppressors was inspiring to me.

"You look peaky," she said while filling one of the large pots with water.

"I think I've got a cold," I said, sniffing loudly to make her believe the lie.

"The only thing to cure a cold is food," she replied, completely seeing through me.

Instead of replying, I dragged a large sack of oatmeal out of the cupboard.

"When was the last time you ate anything?"

I shrugged. "Dunno," I said.

It had been two days. I'd refused to eat porridge with salt in it, fully aware

171

that Father wouldn't feed me anything else, in order to break me. But...like I said...I'm stronger and smarter than any of you give me credit for. I wouldn't have survived those bouts of hunger had you not snuck some chocolate and muffins into my room. As with the birthday doll, I didn't ask how or where you got the food – I simply accepted it.

You saved my life.

Which is why I'm sorry for what I'm about to do.

I talked earlier in this recording about your love of cookery.

And it's true, you *do* love cooking for people.

But there's one thing you never ever cook...or prepare...or make...

Breakfast.

So, what *were* you doing in the kitchen that morning?

TCR 02:27:36:18

This is what happened, as I remember it:

Dorinda left the kitchen so she could have a shower before the morning prayer. Literally a few seconds later, you arrived. Were you waiting for her to leave? Did you know I was there in the kitchen with her? It doesn't matter. The fact is I saw you and you saw me.

You couldn't speak, of course. Because your hands were full.

A bottle of milk in one and in the other...

Insecticide. In a box.

We looked at each other.

You nodded once.

I smiled.

That's all I did as you went to work.

TCR 02:27:59:59

All of our Brothers and Sisters sat at the tables in the church, each with a spoon in their right hand, because use of the left hand is forbidden in the scriptures of Sorak. A shame, because I'm naturally left-handed, or was until Father removed that instinct from me.

172

He stood at the lectern with his coffee and a bowl of steaming hot oatmeal.

Everyone else – Mama Sadie, Mama Dora, Mama Esther, Brother Kenneth, Sister Milly, Brother Linden, Sister Mary-Beth, Sister Joanie, Sister Celestine, Brother Pavel, Brother Jacob, Brother Ethan, Sister Beki, Sister Kimberley, Brother Emir, Sister Indigo, Sister Morag, Brother Rory, Brother Tahir, Brother Bryce, you and me – waited patiently for Sister Dorinda to dole helpings of oatmeal into each bowl.

The smell made my empty belly grumble in disgust.

What was his lecture about that morning?

Oh yes, he was reading from Volume Two of *The Iconic Black Books*. You know, the passage about shoelaces. Goodness knows why he chose that of all chapters to read, but there you have it. Shoelaces. Sorak has **a lot** to say on the topic of shoelaces.

Only your granny can untangle a knotted shoelace. Sorak is your granny. You are the shoelace.

We sat at our tables, waiting for Father to stop talking, each syllable a century in a cold climate. Our porridge was cold too. Not that it made a difference to me. I wouldn't be eating a single bite of it. I'd have to be force-fed again if Father expected me to put even one soggy lump near my lips.

Finally – at last – he concluded his sermon.

"You can now receive the gift of food from Sorak The Almighty!"

Reluctantly everyone in the room lifted their spoons and swallowed their first bite.

"Remember!" Father yelled. "You must have extra salt just like me!"

But he didn't have salt in the little shaker beside his lectern. I should know because I tested it one day. It was sugar. He was a hypocrite and a liar to the very end.

Everybody in the hall became more comfortable in eating their breakfast.

You and me though. Our spoons didn't move off the table.

My eyes scanned the room until they met those of Sister Mary-Beth, the youngest in our church.

Soggy oatmeal was on her lips as she grinned, proud to have finished before everyone.

It was Brother Linden who felt the effect of the poison first.

Everybody stopped to watch as he shot up out of his chair, letting it clatter onto the floor. Linden, eyes nearly popping out of his face, clawed at his throat, leaving red trails on the surface alongside thick veins trying to break out from beneath the skin. He screamed long and loud. Something in his throat *burst*, causing a dirty red flood of partially digested food to cascade from between his lips. Some of it splattered my breakfast, but I didn't move a muscle. All of me was rooted to the chair in grim fascination as events bolted towards their inevitable ugly conclusion.

"What is happening?" Father yelled from above everyone. "Who dares interrupt me?"

"Something's wrong with Linden!" Pavel called out in his accented English.

Linden exposed bloody red teeth, a nasty parody of a smile.

Then he toppled over and died.

Silence.

That silence was followed by a muffled sniffle as Mary-Beth burst into tears.

Then it started all over again with different members of the family.

Father backed away from his lectern.

In that moment he knew what was about to happen.

He made it past my table when the poisoned porridge took effect.

When I next looked over at Sister Mary-Beth, she was gone.

Then the others died the same way Linden did.

All of this took less than three minutes altogether.

The police took slightly longer to arrive, but they came and found us together.

We were waiting for them.

You said nothing, of course.

I waved at the boys in blue.

TCR 02:28:48:51

174

79
21 Jump Street

Uncle Ezra's death didn't upset me too much. Is that a terrible thing to admit? Well it's true. Sorak preaches that we shouldn't speak ill of the dead. Yet doesn't He also preach the value of absolute honesty in Volume Three? I believe the quote is:

It doesn't pay to lie…unless you're lying to the taxman. Ker-ching!

Imelda remained a selfish, vain, arrogant monster. She'd probably fry a vegan meal in real butter and serve it to animal rights activists out of spite, that's her kind of personality. But did she somehow cause Uncle Ezra's death? She looked just as surprised as anyone to see him at the bottom of that staircase when we all found him.

It was around this point that I started to think perhaps Ezra had simply stumbled and had fallen down the stairs by accident. It made more sense, I told myself.

Maybe I tried too hard.

TCR 02:30:16:11

Do you want to know something funny? I had the entire police force of Morvern watching me. Worse, they were *stalking* me at school. There was even a new girl from Class 5C who looked about thirty but dressed like Cassie Trendy.

Undercover cop alert?

She was really friendly to me though. It was a nice novelty, I can't lie.

TCR 02:30:49:59

"Hello," she said as I headed towards the toilet cubicle in PE.

"Hello," I muttered in return.

"I'm Loleene," she smiled, "I'm the new girl at Morvern." Loleene's hair was dyed cherry-red with streaks of black through it, like Marilyn Manson on the *Mechanical Animals* cover art. Dan has that album on her All-Time Favourites list. It was probably intentional on *their* part. Give the undercover copper a weird name so we'd bond and become best friends. Then – and this is probably what they intended – we'd talk, and I'd tell her all my secrets. I have so many secrets. Too many. They wanted me to admit 'my part' in Aimee's accident and confess to Ezra's death.

Do they think I'm naïve? Stupid?

TCR 02:31:58:59

'Loleene' kept trying hard to become my best friend. It became ridiculous. I couldn't go for lunch without her trying to pay for my food. She was there moaning about Aimee, and why she deserved to be pushed down those escalators. During History lessons, I'd be working, only to find that 'Loleene' had passed me some handwritten notes with My Chemical Romance lyrics. She'd done her homework in more ways than one, that's for sure. She was a Don Broco fan, telling me at great length how much she loved Rob. She misquoted lyrics from *Weirdo* by Vukovi at me. Shirley Manson was her 'all-time fave'. Her attempts to create a bridge between us failed consistently because I'd detonate any bridge with an acid comment, or correct her lack of knowledge. I'd invent bands on the spot, improvising marvellously, only for 'Loleene' to tell me she loved those bands too.

I told her:

"My favourite You Me At Six song is *Revenge Fantasy*."

"Mine too!"

There's no such song in their back catalogue.

Eventually my clone's patience evaporated.

"What's your problem?" 'Loleene' yelled at me one day during Domestic Science.

"Entrapment," I said quietly, while whisking some eggs in a big white bowl.

"Huh?"

She hadn't heard me.

"Entrapment!" I repeated, louder this time, hoping she didn't think it was a song title.

My classmates looked around at us, nervously watching from nearby.

'Loleene' heard me that time. I know because her face paled until it was the same colour as the ceramic bowl that was sitting snugly on my forearm. My soufflé would be nice.

"Tell Guthrie he's got the wrong idea about me," I added, further explaining myself.

'Loleene' didn't answer.

Instead she turned and walked out of Homeroom 2C.

'Loleene' didn't graduate from Morvern High School…because she never existed.

80

We Need To Talk About Imelda

Rhona glared balefully at me every time we passed in the corridors or sat nearby in class. My body stiffened in her presence; trapped tension that could find no release. It frustrated me that she had escaped punishment for what she'd done to Dan in life and death. Manipulating Sasha into sorting out Aimee had been easy, but as a result I'd drawn attention to myself. For all intents and purposes, Rhona was protected.

If anything happened to her, it would make me look guilty.

It wasn't as though I didn't have other problems to sort out.

This brings me to the next part of my story.

We need to talk about Imelda.

TCR 02:33:15:50

Aren't you even the slightest bit curious why she left last week? I hope she stays gone, quite frankly. She's a bad sort, Aunt Imelda. I've always known – since the moment I laid eyes on her at the school gates – that something wasn't quite right. Everything she did and said – including the words *Hello* and *my name is Imelda* – felt like a really phony performance. She is a liar of Brobdingnagian proportions. If only her wit was Swift!

You don't know why she left so suddenly in the middle of the night.

I do.

Here's what happened.

There I was in my bedroom, lying on my bed with the TV on during a blazing hot day, watching reruns of *Poldark*, when a rousing speech from Ross Poldark was suddenly interrupted by knocking at my door. I thought back to Inspector Guthrie, but it definitely wasn't him: the knocks weren't loud enough.

It had to be Imelda.

"What is it?" I shouted, my good mood turning sour.

"Hello, my darling," Imelda cooed from behind the door.

I didn't want to entertain her idiocy.

"Get whizzed," I called back, hurling my latest insult that I'd invented to avoid swearing.

"You really do need to be very nice to me," Aunt Imelda continued in her breathy voice, "because I've solved the riddle and you need to listen to what I have to say."

I froze and re-evaluated my initial stance.

Incidentally, *re-evaluate* gave me an extra point in my last vocab test.

"Come in."

Aunt Imelda's face glowed with smugness, or fake tan. It was impossible to tell which.

"Hey girl," Imelda said, poking her head from behind my half-opened door, "I wanted to talk to you about the dead Deacon's riddle. Turns out it was far easier than I realised. I've spent weeks hunting for the answer only to suddenly realise the truth!"

She paused, then spoke again:

"Do you want to know the answer?"

I smiled wearily, but remained silent and worried.

"The answer is…"

She thrust something at me.

A plastic box that once contained a copy of *The Women*.

"But you already know it, don't you?"

"No."

"Oh Starrsha, my dear, don't play dumb with me. It won't work. You see there's a phrase that you won't find in any of the *Iconic Black Books of Sorak The Almighty*. Do you want to hear it? Of course you do." (I didn't.) "It goes like this: you can't kid a kidder."

Imelda walked into my room and loomed threateningly over me as I sat cross-legged on my bed with a *Sweet Valley High* book in my hands. She was dressed in a Debbie Harry T-shirt, ripped to expose her belly. Her skirt was black leather, matching her heels.

She looked every bit the *femme fatale* of Father's favourite films.

"Where is it?"

My heart pounded irregularly and I felt my chest tighten.

"I don't know what you mean."

"You trifling little brat! I won't ask again. Where is it? The Deacon left a key in this cassette box and you've got it!"

TCR 02:34:45:20

The reason Father had summoned Imelda back home was so we'd all squabble and fight over his fortune. His hints, clues and inconsistent stories were all part of his plot. Everything had been leading up to this point in my life. I knew one thing above all else:

Father wanted us to fight. That's why he reunited you and me with Imelda and Ezra.

I bet he expected the entire congregation to turn on each other in his absence.

But he underestimated your cunning.

TCR 02:35:00:00

"Give me the key!"

"No!" I yelled hotly.

"So you *do* have it!"

Before I could react, Imelda leaned down and grabbed my wrist tightly. She twisted hard, burning my skin with friction. I screamed in pain. Then I slammed my copy of *Slam Book Fever* – Number 48 in the *Sweet Valley High* series in case you're interested – into her face with enough force to make her recoil in pain. She released my wrist and I fled my bedroom in terror.

"You won't escape me!" Imelda screeched behind me.

"You won't escape the fashion police," I shouted back.

"I'll kill her," she snarled aloud, telling herself what she wanted to do to me.

I resisted the overpowering urge to scream your name. You wouldn't have heard my voice anyway. But instinct pushed me to find you – to give you a chance to save me from the monster we'd been living with for the last few months. Imelda's heels click-clacked on the floor as I bolted down from the upstairs balcony, heading towards the lower level of The Sanctum as quickly as I could manage.

She chased me downstairs. I froze at the top of the staircase that led down, down, down to the basement level. Uncle Ezra's body had landed at the bottom of that same staircase. But I wanted to get into The Secret Cinema and lock the door. There were other locked rooms in the house, like the one with the red door, but I didn't have keys to any of them.

Instead I moved in the opposite direction towards…

…the front door.

"Give me that key!" Imelda yelled.

"Give me a break!" I retorted.

"That can be arranged. Your neck or your legs?"

I pushed out into the hissing rain and ran away from The Sanctum, towards the river.

81

I've Got The Key
(I've Got The Secret)

Imelda followed me outside into the downpour, pursuing me relentlessly in a pair of heels that didn't seem to slow her down. She probably couldn't move properly without a bit of height; she was so used to her Louboutins that a pair of sensible flat shoes would probably have caused her to spiral into depression. It didn't matter if she caught up with me anyway, because I only needed to reach the river on the edge of the estate.

"Give me my damn key, you heinous little bitch!"

'Bitch' wasn't nice and I've never approved of it, but Father once announced that the word *bitch* wasn't bad. Sister Dorinda had berated him for his liberal use of the word against women. Smugly, he informed her that he was actually **complimenting** his wives when he called them 'his bitches'. After all, didn't Sorak The Almighty state:

A bitch is actually a Beautiful Individual That Creates Haters.

So why didn't I feel like Imelda was using the word in the same spirit as *The Iconic Books* suggested? I huffed and puffed as the rain beat down on me, my hair an affront to everything Cassie Trendy stood for in this world. My fringe stuck to my eyes, covering a good part of my peripheral vision. But I knew Imelda was close and would hotly pursue me until she got what she wanted. And what she wanted was in my left trouser pocket.

Finally, we both reached the river.

I stood on the edge of the gushing torrent, seething in sympathy with the stormy weather. It looked ferocious and powerful; a suitable backdrop to a final confrontation, like Holmes and Moriarty and The Reichenbach Falls. I'd be

Sherlock, of course.

Honestly, the only thing missing was dramatic thunder and lightning.

"I won't ask again," Imelda gasped.

I thrust my hand into my right trouser pocket and produced a little key.

Her eyes lit up at the sight of it. She said:

"The old Deacon has a fortune in tax-free money stashed away in several accounts. But no-one knows where to find them. There's a box in the bank with all the papers and forms. I need to access that money. The Deacon left a modern-day treasure map!"

That's what she told me. I wonder if she'd said anything to you.

I raised the key and made to hand it over, letting her get a long look at it.

She reached out eagerly, hopeful.

Then…before she could stop me…

I swung my arm upwards and launched the key into the river.

Imelda screamed as the little key disappeared into the rushing dirty water.

"You'll never find it. That river runs faster than you in a pair of high heels."

She looked at me with an expression of pure undiluted hatred.

But I like to think there was a hint of respect too.

Aunt Imelda said nothing else to me. She turned and slunk off back to the house.

It was cold and wet but I wanted to stay near the river for a few extra seconds, if only to marvel at the sheer power and force within the churning waters.

Then I reached into my left trouser pocket and felt for the little key.

It was still there, and there it has remained ever since.

And the key I threw into the river?

It was the key for my locker at school.

82

Something Quiet And Creepy

If I thought my life would go back to being the way it was before Father sent those videotapes (along with Aunt and Uncle) then I was deeply mistaken. Life isn't like this videotape you're watching. You can't just rewind and replay. It's impossible.

You were sullen and barely around while I was lonely and frustrated.

The police were all but harassing me, but they weren't the only ones forcing themselves into my life. The scumbag pretending to be Sorak The Almighty started calling me again, trying to provoke me into making a fool of myself. *The closest you'll ever get to being kissed is the kiss of death*, read one of the messages, the plain font doing nothing to dull the vicious sentiment behind the words. Another said: *Inspector Guthrie knows you were responsible for Aimee's 'accident'. He knows because I sent him a vision in a dream.* That private message was slightly more menacing because the sender seemed to know I was connected to what happened at the Theatre Royal.

It didn't matter.

I still had a pile of *Sweet Valley High* books to get through.

They were my constant companions every night as I lay on my bed in silence.

TCR 02:37:05:39

It was whilst reading *Wrong Kind Of Girl* (Number 10 in the series) that I heard something that I shouldn't have heard. I gently placed the book on my lap and cocked my ear towards the floor. It happened again. A lone sound in the silence. It wasn't you. You'd gone out into town to buy groceries. You'd been leaving the house a lot to do little tasks like shopping or paying bills. At first I thought the silence was playing tricks on my ears, but I'd definitely heard something far away that had carried up to my bedroom through the old wooden floors and concrete walls. If I hadn't been reading about Elizabeth and Jessica, I wouldn't have heard…

Footsteps.

Definitely footsteps.

Faint but firm.

83

Ghost House

Do you believe in ghosts? I don't. But I started to think the old house might have a few moving around the rooms at night. Don't get me wrong, the house had always been…unquiet…but I usually blamed Aunt Imelda. I blamed her for everything. Maybe she was an easy target, a convenient scapegoat?

I decided the only way to solve this mystery was to go on a ghost hunt.

TCR 02:37:53:59

84

The Red Door

I swung my legs around and dropped off my bed, landing gently on the carpeted floor. I felt the fibres beneath my feet as I crept into the hall. The sound of footsteps hadn't come from above, which meant they were from below. I moved towards the staircase and tip-toed down, going to great pains in order to maintain silence.

It played on my mind that perhaps Father and our Family had returned for revenge. But they would come after you, because you're the one who poisoned them, not me.

Then I shoved that theory out of my head and proceeded with a more realistic one:

That that cow Imelda was back and hiding in the house.

"You'll get the back of my hand," I whispered, repeating not one of Sorak's quotes but one from Father, the same he used whenever one of The Family got out of line.

The sound of movement seemed to stop as I made my way down to the basement of the house. The Secret Cinema was along the hallway, as was Father's office. The red door, tantalisingly locked, was at its other end. I crossed it in a few steps.

Leaning down, I peered through the keyhole of the red door and saw the black room for the first time. Why did I call it the black room? Because everything inside is painted black: the walls, the furniture, the floor...all of it.

My inquisitiveness made me push a little closer in an attempt to see more.

A shadow stood in front of the other side of the keyhole, blocking the view.

The empty room painted completely in black wasn't empty.

85

The Invisible Intruder

My first instinct was to shout at the intruder behind the locked door, but my slyness kicked in. There was no point in letting the intruder know I was aware of their presence. Instead, I crept back upstairs into the main wing of the house. Father used to keep spare keys for the locked doors. He kept them in the broom closet. It was a dirty little cupboard with lashings of thick dust and asbestos panelling. With my face covered by one of my hands, I reached into the dusty darkness and grabbed a large set of rusty keys with my free hand. Then I rushed back to the staircase that lead downstairs.

A few seconds later I stood outside the red door that led into the black room.

Gently, with shaking fingers, I slotted a key into the lock.

It didn't turn.

The next key was just as useless.

The third key, however, turned smoothly.

TCR 02:38:19:59

86

My Rent-Free Tenant

The black room was empty by the time I got through the door. There was a second door at the opposite end. Perhaps it led to a white room? There was a secret wing of the house I hadn't explored. Imagine that! Anyway, my feet took me across the black room, each footstep leaving an imprint in the black carpet. The furniture in the room was minimalist but chic. The black room had a nasty oppressive atmosphere, uniquely its own. Why was it painted black? Was there a reason? What had it been used for?

All this and more flashed through my brain as I negotiated my way to the other door.

I hadn't even touched the handle when I heard a voice on the other side.

You know what I'm going to say, don't you?

Course you do.

I recognised that voice. It stirred up old memories.

It wasn't until I peered through the crack of the almost-open door that I put a face to the voice. It belonged to someone I had not seen for years.

TCR 02:39:37:05

"You promised me she'd be dead," the voice said smoothly, "and she's still here causing problems. I want her dealt with once and for all. If you love me, you'll kill her."

Several seconds passed before I realised the voice was talking about *me*.

"Kill her!" the voice repeated. "If you want me, you've got to please me."

"Kill her!"

"Kill the interfering brat!"

"Kill Starrsha like you killed all the others!"

The voice was a low whisper now as it urged violence and death upon me.

I peeked through the crack of the door to see…

Yes. **You**.

Why were you there, Simon?

But the voice didn't belong to you, obviously. That's why it sounded like a one-way conversation. Someone was talking and you were responding with fingers that I could only just see. I wish I hadn't.

I CAN'T KILL HER RIGHT NOW.

TOO RISKY.

WE'LL DO IT SOON.

I'LL MAKE IT LOOK LIKE SUICIDE.

My heart broke at your betrayal, but *her* betrayal somehow felt worse.

One of the few good memories I had of my childhood now felt soiled.

It was Miss Gibson, my ex-tutor.

87

Reviewing The Situation

It explained a lot of things that I'd always questioned but never quite understood. For instance, how were you able to get me a birthday doll and other items from the outside world when you hadn't stepped past the gates? Father ruthlessly controlled access, but you were always able to sidestep his barriers and smuggle stuff into the estate.

And now I knew how.

You had a source on the outside.

Not just a source.

A lover.

The sound of kissing was loud enough for me to hear, even from behind the black door.

Was it love at first sight?

How did you first tell her you loved her?

Was it with fingers?

Or actions?

Was it with flowers?

Or did you prove your love by slaughtering everyone in the Church?

The motive is money, isn't it?

The key is right here. This is how you get the money.

But you'll never have it.

Neither will Miss Gibson.

Not anymore.

88

Forgiveness

Have you any idea what I've done for you? How far I've gone to protect your secret?

I only did what I did because I thought you'd rescued me from Father. I assumed it was all to save me from him. And you, of course, wanted to be free. Maybe I've been lying to myself. It wouldn't be the first time. You killed *everyone*. I thought…maybe…you didn't mean to kill the others. They were collateral damage in your bid to kill Father.

You intended to kill me too.

For her!

TCR 02:41:10:05

89

What I've Done For You

Earlier, I said this recording was…a message, or a prayer.

But this is neither a message nor a prayer.

It's a confession.

Yes, you've lied to me all along. But I've lied as well. I'm still lying. It's almost pathological at this point. It's wrong. I told you that I wanted this to be a truthful account of what happened – how we ended up where we are now. It's only right that I tell you everything. When I discovered you and Miss Gibson together, it broke me.

I've been near the edge for so long.

It was the final push.

I'm falling free!

Dear Dan.

I killed her.

I did it all for you.

TCR 02:42:39:50

90

Rhona's Party (Reprise)

It was the first – and last – time I'd been drunk. The feeling of alcohol in my blood made me sick and weak. My arms and legs wobbled, it felt like fire flowing through my veins. Dan and I were talking and...what did I say earlier...I said *I told her everything*. That wasn't a lie. We were at Rhona's party and the wine loosened my lips, lowered my protective barrier. Dan, my best friend, was there for me and I blurted it all out:

"It was Simon. He poisoned everyone. He did it."

Dan didn't react. Not at first. But it didn't take long for her to understand the implications of my confession. Her face revealed her feelings in fine detail: horror, disbelief, and finally...fear.

"You've got to tell the police," she told me.

"Nah," I slurred, the wine soaking my brain in that boozy bath I mentioned earlier.

"He killed twenty people in cold blood."

"Twenty-three, actually."

"It isn't funny, Starrsha!"

A few minutes later Rhona came for Dan at the party. She showed everyone the love letter Dan had entrusted to me to give to Aimee, the one that had been stolen.

Except...

91

Loose Lips Sink Relationships

Dan's secret letter to Aimee wasn't stolen.

You can't know what it's like to be a girl in a world that resists your every attempt to fit in with the in-crowd. I wanted to go to Rhona's party so badly I actually felt it in my guts. If I went to her party, life would improve. If people saw me at her house, they'd like me. You have to understand that Dan was going to announce her relationship with Aimee at the party. She wouldn't need me anymore. I wanted to be happy for my friend, but I was terrified she'd abandon me for Princess Perfect Face.

Her face isn't so perfect now, not since it met the escalator stairs.

Simon, I would have done *anything* to get an invitation to Rhona's party.

That's why I handed Dan's letter to Rhona in return for an invite.

Do you understand now?

Do you realise the full extent of my lies?

I betrayed my best friend for a crappy party.

And after I betrayed her, I killed her.

TCR 02:43:17:39

Dan helped me back into our taxi, but she didn't want to leave the party. She seemed troubled by the whole experience. Aimee had been pressured by Rhona and her friends into scorning Dan in public. Both this and my confession rattled my best friend. She wasn't getting into a taxi with me. Instead she bundled me into the back of the cab and staggered back up the path. I was too drunk to do much. As the taxi pulled out of Rhona's driveway, I saw Dan fall to the ground, gracelessly falling on her butt.

I told you earlier that the journey to Rhona's house took ten minutes in the cab.

But I messed up when I said it took me *forty minutes* to get back home from the party.

You must have realised that my account of that night didn't make sense. It's true. I stopped the taxi and headed back on foot. The night air and the growing realisation I'd told Dan too much sobered me quickly. She was still in Rhona's driveway, alone in the freezing cold, drunk and tired. I might have been tipsy, but I wasn't tired. That was what really did it for Dan. She was propped up against a tree, hidden at the corner of Rhona's garden. Hazily, she looked up at me.

"I'm cold," she murmured.

"It's a cold night," I responded.

Her eyelids drooped until it was impossible for her to keep them open. Dan tried, she really did, but the alcohol and the cold beat her into submission. For a few seconds I reconsidered my actions, because she was my best friend.

Best friends *should* stick together.

However, she knew too much. My own fault, but Dan now posed a threat to everything we'd been through. Why did I do it? What made me drop my guard?

Dan's last word was a simple one:

"Goodnight."

My last word to her was likewise simple:

"Goodbye."

Then she froze to death.

92

Life Is Disappointing

I killed my best friend for you.
  And all along you were lying to me.
  How disappointing.

TCR 02:45:10:01

93

Whoops!

Time turned against me. It was only a matter of weeks, possibly days, before Miss Gibson and you made a move. I refused to eat anything you prepared; past experience having taught me that you'd attempt to use poison. What was your plan? Perhaps you'd tell the police I was responsible for all the poisonings and Uncle Ezra's death?

Uncle Ezra. He must have been surprised to see Miss Gibson behind him at the top of the staircase. She pushed him, of course. Who else could it have been? I guarantee she held the study door shut while Uncle Ezra assaulted me with that steel poker.

This has been going on for years, hasn't it?

Do you know what Sorak The Almighty has to say on the subject of betrayal?

If you cross the wrong person, they'll be very cross.

You sold us out for a woman! Yes, Miss Gibson is beautiful. But Aimee taught me that beautiful people can be untrustworthy and backstabbing. My vendetta towards Aimee, Rhona, and the rest of them might sound misplaced now that I've admitted to letting Dan freeze to death, but I still blame them for everything bad that happened at school.

Aimee is lucky. Why? Because I let her live.

If I'd wanted her dead, I'd have pushed harder.

Whoops!

I nearly forgot to tell you.

Did you honestly believe all that nonsense about Sasha Jenkins doing it?

94

A Late Night Out/
A Violent Night In

Miss Gibson became my next target and you were too clueless to stop me.

I'd been extremely patient and knew exactly what I wanted to do, but you were annoyingly persistent. You wouldn't leave the house. If I had a girlfriend, or a boyfriend (I'm not sure) living in another part of the house, I'd probably want to stay at home all day every day too.

Then, one day, you finally had to leave the house for the day.

Better still…you wouldn't be back until late.

TCR 02:46:18:41

There I was in bed, reading *Outcast* (Number 41 in the *Sweet Valley High* series), when I heard the main door slam shut. Untangling myself from my bedsheets, I leapt up and over to my window. You were down by the swimming pool, walking the path towards the gates. Unless there was a secret entrance outside, you were definitely leaving the estate.

I'M GOING TO THE LAWYER'S OFFICE, THEN THE FARMER'S MARKET, you'd told me during the previous night's dinner. I WON'T BE BACK UNTIL LATE.

Unbeknownst to you, I'd already tipped my plate of macaroni cheese into the bin.

Why take a chance?

You didn't notice my happy expression. Why would you? You were too busy forking pieces of soft pasta soaked with gloopy cheese into your mouth. But I felt it – happiness, real happiness, was the light on my face. I hadn't smiled in so long, not since I'd met Dan.

You're probably asking yourself: why was my 'sister' smiling?

Because with you gone for the day, I could *finally* put my plan into action.

Now you're really scared.

95
The Writing's On The Wall

The staircase to the lower level of the house had never looked so foreboding. The lights were off, leaving everything in a gloomy default state. You obviously didn't want me down there, which is understandable considering someone was living downstairs.

Not for much longer.

TCR 02:47:50:41

I descended into the lower levels of The Sanctum, walking until I reached the red door at the far end of the hall. I'd expected to find it locked. In actual fact it was unlocked. Did she leave it open on purpose? Yes, I think so. Maybe she knew I'd started to suspect something. What gave me away? The fact that I refused to eat the food you prepared? The way I refused to cling to you like floating debris in the sea?

I don't care. The door was open and the path was clear. It saved me a lot of trouble.

Cautiously, I entered the black room, closing the red door behind me. The smell of the room – musty before – was now vile and putrid. I gagged and backed away momentarily. The stench stimulated a memory of dead people over tables, with oatmeal and blood all over their lips and faces. But this was much stronger, more forceful. I coughed and covered my nostrils, trying to block out the stench.

Something caught my attention. It hadn't been in the room during my last visit.

It was on the wall, scrawled in fresh white paint, with dripping trails falling towards the skirting board. It was a message of some sort, made starkly visible by the black canvass behind it. My eyes strained in the gloom, but soon they would see well enough to interpret the words as only I understood them.

It was a quote from Volume Two of Sorak The Almighty's *Iconic Black Books*:

The deadliest enemy in the world is a girl with secrets.

It was aimed at me, obviously. It didn't matter to me, because I only wanted to confront your girlfriend. With this very much in mind, I turned to walk into the next room and find her...but I found something else instead. It was another new addition to the black room that hadn't been there last time.

I hadn't noticed it at first, because the words on the wall had distracted me.

But the gross smell should have made me realise sooner.

It lay propped up on a small white plastic chair.

Battered and bloody, it was quite dead.

I peered closer...

It was Aunt Imelda, with a pitchfork sticking out of her chest.

As I screamed a shrill, throat-shredding cry of horror, someone laughed.

"Child," a kindly voice said from nearby, "come to me and receive your blessing."

96

The Secret Of Glowglass

Imelda hadn't managed to leave the estate after all.

Did she know about your relationship with Miss Gibson? Were you all in on it together? Stupid, irritating, vicious Imelda with her voice like a drowning bag of cats and her wardrobe so hideous that even Victoria's Secret would try to keep it secret. She really misunderstood you, didn't she? Just like me. Just like all of us.

"Child," the voice from the next room said once again, "are you coming to see me, or do you just want to stand around staring at the recently departed?"

Hastily, I moved away from the decaying body and into the next room.

TCR 02:49:59:59

It wasn't painted black, which immediately put me at ease. I couldn't completely relax in the presence of a person I'd once worshipped as zealously as I do Sorak The Almighty. She sat reclining on a winged armchair with green tartan fabric on the soft cushion. The walls were painted in a similar style, with a tartan effect completely at odds with the stark dark of the black room. The wall behind her had a fireplace built into it, but it was unlit. The carpet beneath my feet was cream-coloured with black zigzags.

It was a nice little nest for lovers.

"I decorated it myself," she said, her wide, pleasant eyes blinking at me.

No wonder you fell in love with her.

It almost worked on me too.

Miss Gibson still looked as beautiful as when she used to sit with me in the kitchen with books sprawled across the table, Father sitting across from us, staring intently, looking for hints of subversion or corruption.

He looked in the wrong place, didn't he?

Father should have been keeping a closer eye on you and Miss Gibson.

TCR 02:48:10:50

"Why?" I asked.

"You know why," she replied, sipping from a white porcelain cup.

"Money?"

"Love," she replied, with a scrunched expression of surprise.

"With everyone out the way, you and Simon can have the entire fortune to yourselves."

Miss Gibson tilted her head, lengthening her long neck until her chestnut hair fell across her shoulders. She was beautiful, but she was also a poser. Why hadn't I seen that before? She lay there unhurried, dressed in a vintage ruffled nightgown.

"You look like a glamourous old movie star," I said.

Miss Gibson laughed. It was a pretty laugh.

"It was how I got the job as your tutor."

TCR 02:49:00:09

For a brief second, a quick interlude, I wondered whether or not Miss Gibson had planned to infiltrate The Church of Sorak The Almighty from the very start. Father was many things: vain, greedy, childish, evil, kind, vindictive… but he wasn't stupid.

It occurred to me that it was possible Miss Gibson had been fed information in order to get herself past the gates and into The Sanctum, close to Father.

But how close?

Yuck.

TCR 02:49:47:29

"Deacon Randolph Glowglass was a vain show-off," Miss Gibson explained.

"You're being far too polite," I replied.

"One day, after your lesson, he brought me down here to sign a cheque.

While signing it, he opened a drawer in that desk over there…" She motioned towards an old oak desk like the one in his office. "He lifted out a brick of brown banknotes tied with string."

Her eyes shone at that memory until another memory darkened her expression.

"I planted death threats from Sorak The Almighty in the same drawer. Your father was paranoid, like all rich men in power. He was right to be scared though. You were all stashed up here in this place, cut off from reality, with the rest of us struggling to live through austerity and the sort of poverty you'll *never* comprehend. You don't know what it's like to be poor, to have your mother cry because she can't afford to feed you and your family. You'll never have to raid supermarket bins for your breakfast. I saw that money in the drawer and knew I wanted it for myself. Simon wanted me to be happy. He suggested we kill everyone and take the money."

TCR 02:50:41:02

I had to hear it for myself.

You weren't just part of her scheme.

You were behind the whole thing.

TCR 02:51:04:38

97

Books And Crooks

There were still a few questions I needed Miss Gibson to answer, if only because I really didn't understand everything. Besides, time was running away from me. I had to get everything sorted before you returned. If you came back too soon, then my plans would be screwed. Praise Sorak for lawyers and overcomplicated legal matters.

The first question to be asked was also the quickest to be answered:

"Did you kill Uncle Ezra?"

"Yes," Miss Gibson said with a slight shrug of her shoulders.

"You wanted me to look guilty in front of Inspector Guthrie."

"Not quite," she said, "but that was a neat twist in the tale."

"Huh?"

"Your senile uncle saw me coming out from the red door and he waited at the top of the staircase. The commotion upstairs made me careless, because I'm terribly nosy and want to know everything. Anyway, my plan to eavesdrop on you and the others was spoiled by Ezra. What a nutter! He told me I was evil…"

"He was telling you the truth," I said grudgingly.

"He said he'd tell the police an intruder had broken into the house. He thought I was a burglar. But there was a real danger he'd expose me, and that would expose your brother too. Everything we'd planned would be for nothing. That's why I kicked the old goat down the stairs."

"And ran off before anyone could see you," I said. "It made the police realise something weird was happening in this house."

"Ezra would have been disposed of regardless." Miss Gibson sipped from her cup. "He'd just been made the major beneficiary of The Deacon's last will and testament."

My next question brought back memories of bruises gone but not forgotten.

"Did you lock me in the study with him?"

"Yes. I was out and about the house that day. I had to be careful. But I couldn't resist pulling the door shut and leaving you in there with Ezra."

"You tried to kill me," I said dumbly. Even though I knew what Miss Gibson was capable of doing, it still felt intrinsically wrong that my beloved tutor was a conniving murderess. Maybe I'd learned more from her than I actually realised?

"Yes, I wanted you dead." she replied.

There wasn't a shred of remorse in that woman.

I may have killed my best friend for you, but no-one will ever tell me I don't regret it.

It was time for another question.

"Have you been pretending to be Sorak The Almighty?"

Miss Gibson covered her face with a bedazzled hand, her engagement ring catching me off-guard. I didn't know, of course. You kept an entire part of your life so secret.

Would it have killed you to tell me?

Miss Gibson uncovered her face, straightened her posture, and bellowed:

"You must not defy the power of Sorak The Almighty!"

It was the voice on the other side of my iPhone.

I trembled slightly in fear, but also budding anger.

"It's all nonsense anyway," she said dismissively.

It *is* all nonsense. I know. But it's in my brain. I believe, and I hate myself for it.

"You shouldn't mock someone's religious beliefs," I said huffily.

"Have you actually read those stupid *Black Books* of Sorak? I was so bored I took time to study them and…"

"And?"

"None of it makes the slightest bit of sense!"

"I live my life by the advice in those books."

"And what an exciting life you lead as a result," Miss Gibson said sympathetically.

My anger was now reaching a point of no return.

Miss Gibson had to die.

It would be like slaying a dragon or staking a vampire.

There's nothing in any of the *Iconic Black Books* warning against killing a gold-digger.

Weirdly, she saw something in my eyes that alerted her to my intention.

Perhaps it was similar to what she saw in the mirror every morning?

"You came here to kill me," she said in the voice of Sorak, booming and dramatic.

"No," I lied.

"You want me dead!"

"I don't!"

"You came here to kill me and you want me dead!" She stood up from the chair and moved menacingly towards me. "I'll finish what your Uncle Ezra started."

Her dainty hand wrapped itself around a steel poker sitting discarded near the fireplace behind the upholstered tartan chair. My eyes followed her as she tensed for a fight.

"It's time for you to join your Family in whatever afterlife you believe in…"

Then, with a violent scream, Miss Gibson swung the poker and charged right at me.

98

The Final Battle

It was surreal to see my old tutor swinging a steel poker whilst dressed in an expensive nightgown. But not so odd that I didn't have time to turn and run for my life. As I reached the door into the black room, I grabbed the edge of the oak table and threw it over, toppling the desk and its contents onto the floor.

As the desk fell, it slammed into Miss Gibson's left leg, slicing downwards until blood flowed. She cried out in pain, but didn't stop to check her wound. While she negotiated the fallen table, I darted past Imelda's corpse, leaving the black room through the red door, emerging into the downstairs hall.

"Sorak commands you to stay and die with dignity!"

"How dumb do you think I am?" I shouted back, but my voice wavered. I could run faster than anyone, but running and holding a discussion wasn't really my thing.

Miss Gibson made it to the top of the staircase, the poker still in her hand.

I came out of hiding and punched her in the chest.

Her face twisted in furious surprise as she fell backwards.

She tumbled down the steep stairs, with her steel poker rolling down step-by-step. It clattered to a rest on the threadbare carpet where Uncle Ezra's body had lain after Miss Gibson had done to him what I had just done to her.

Unfortunately, Miss Gibson was far more resilient than my ancient uncle.

Shakily, but undeniably alive, she climbed back onto her feet.

Her hand grasped at the poker again until it was firmly in her grip.

"I'm going to force-feed you a bowl of delicious hot oatmeal," she snarled.

"I don't like salt."

As a witty comeback, it lacked...well, wit.

But it was all I had at that point. That and my legs. No long words from the Vocab Test. No wise quotes. My legs took me out of Miss Gibson's reach. Every time she got close, they put me farther away. I'd managed to run all the way back to Rhona's house on the night of her party. Even though I was slightly worse for wear, I still got there so I could greet my best friend for the final time. No-one realised quite how fast I could run when I concentrated.

I knew my speed would help me once again. But I had to think as fast as my legs worked; otherwise Miss Gibson would get me.

It soon dawned on me there was only one thing I could do.

TCR 02:54:39:58

You already know, don't you?

It's the reason you can't find her in the house.

It's also the reason I'm covered in blood.

You need to know what I did to your fiancé.

I want you to know in detail how I killed her.

TCR 02:54:41:40

We took our fight into the kitchen.

A kitchen is actually quite a useful place if you're running for your life. I darted around the table, putting it between us, making Miss Gibson chase me. She couldn't quite get close enough to use her weapon. Every now and again she'd lunge from the other end, slamming the poker off the surface. It hurt her hand quite badly. Silly woman. I launched a few plates in her general direction, hurling them like discuses, shattering each one with vicious precision above her head.

"You little cow," she seethed, "I'll kill you!"

Once I'd run out of plates to smash, I chucked a few cups and mugs at her face.

After the cups and mugs came the saucers.

The saucers were followed by forks and knives.

Then I abandoned the sink and made for the refrigerator.

Unfortunately, this meant I couldn't keep the kitchen table as a barrier between her and me.

Miss Gibson swung the poker with all the strength her upper arm could unleash, narrowly missing my left rib as it swished past me. By then I'd already opened the fridge and found a few glass bottles of wine. They felt nice and heavy in my hand, but trust me – they made excellent projectile weapons. The first bottle sailed through the air until it connected with the wall above Miss Gibson's head.

She was showered in wine and broken glass.

"Get away from me!" I yelled.

The second bottle hit her square on the nose.

Ouch.

The third and final bottle impacted on her chest, sending her reeling into a wall.

Miss Gibson had a weapon – her steel poker similar to the one that had put me in hospital – but my weapon was better. It was greater than any blunt instrument or sharp blade.

It was knowledge.

I knew the upper levels of The Sanctum better than Miss Gibson. She was queen of everything behind the red door, but everything else upstairs belonged to me. I'd lived in this old house when my brothers and sisters had been forced to sleep in a freezing, unfit-for-habitation old dormitory.

This house was mine and *she* was the intruder.

Miss Gibson staggered after me, poker dragging heavily in her right hand. I was too fast and moved up the spiral staircase to the upper level of the house. We met at the balcony that connects the middle hallway to the upper hallway – where my bedroom could be found. I peered over the banister into the middle of the house – the front door visible, as was the stairway down to the lower level.

"I don't think you ever told me your real name," I said quietly as a bedraggled and bloody Miss Gibson closed the gap between herself and me.

"It's Marisol," she said with bloodied lips.

"That's a nice name."

She raised the poker and swung it one final time.

I ducked.

The weight of the weapon took her over the edge of the banister.

Miss Gibson uttered a howl of surprise as she fell.

TCR 02:56:17:10

99

Goodbye Gibson

She lay on the ground near the front door looking utterly graceful in death. It hadn't been the same with Uncle Ezra; he'd landed at an awkward angle after being pushed. Miss Gibson's breaths came alongside pain; and when she exhaled, a fine red mist fluttered out from her mouth. It wouldn't be long before she stopped breathing altogether.

I moved slowly down the spiral stairs from the safety of the balcony.

Her eyes followed me, but even that caused her to grimace.

She still looked beautiful. You would have been proud of her, I know.

Soon enough, I stood over Miss Gibson's inert body.

"Well done," she gasped, "you deserve top marks."

"I'm going to teach Simon a lesson next," I said quietly. I was already thinking of setting up the camcorder so you could come home and watch a special presentation.

As Miss Gibson lay helpless and broken, I leaned down, safe in the knowledge that she wouldn't be able to stop me taking the heavy poker. I unfurled her grip finger-by-finger. Her nails had been recently manicured. They were sharp and even. It was good work.

There I stood, holding the hefty poker experimentally, looking at it intensely.

"You don't know the truth," Miss Gibson said with a sigh of pain. Perhaps the sharp side of a bone had pierced something important in her body?

"What's the truth?" I asked with a smirk.

Not that I cared, because she was a liar through and through.

But I'm glad I listened.

"Your real father…"

"I don't care."

"It isn't Randolph Glowglass…"

"I know."

"You do?"

"We all called him 'Father' as a mark of respect befitting our Church's spiritual leader. He was only related by blood to Ezra and Imelda. I was his adopted daughter."

The sound of gurgling blood wasn't nice to hear, less so once I realised it was laughter.

"You little fool," Miss Gibson croaked, "how could you not know?"

"Know what?"

Then she said it aloud.

Finally.

My response was to raise the poker and ferociously swing it down over and over and over and over and over and over and over again and again and again and again and again and again and again and again and again and again and again and again and again and over and over and over and over and over again.

My body shuddered with exhaustion and other emotional vibrations.

But I had more to do.

This, actually.

TCR 02:58:00:00

100

Confession

Hello, Dad.

I wish you'd told me from the start.

It explains a lot of things I've never understood, except the most important thing:

Why were you planning to kill me?

I wouldn't have told on you.

I love you.

Loved.

I can forgive *anything* except betrayal. Yet I've betrayed everyone in my attempts to protect our life together. I've betrayed Dan, and there's no religious ritual that will absolve that guilt. She was the one person who saw in me something special. And how did I repay her friendship? With disloyalty. I shouldn't have gone against her…but you know better than most that love makes you do screwy things. I'm not talking about what you had with Miss Gibson, I'm talking about a different sort of love, the kind that you find in your best friend.

Ah.

The videotape is nearly done. How many hours have I been talking? You've been watching me for a while, haven't you? The VCR is fine, by the way. It won't chew up this tape. I cleaned it up so you could watch without any problems. Isn't that good? I'm so thoughtful.

This really is the end now.

I have regrets, of course. I'm annoyed that Rhona never got what she deserved. I had so many ideas about how to hurt that girl for what she did to Dan. I regret that I won't get a chance to finish off the whole *Sweet Valley High* collection. What happened to Jessica and Elizabeth? Will they ever stop fighting and realise they're stronger together? And why do they even need boyfriends? Oh, I'll miss them terribly.

Those books made me *so* happy.

What else?

I'm disappointed that I never got the chance to spend all the money 'Father' left behind in the bank. You'll probably already know that the key and all the information have gone. I got rid of the lot. That money is cursed. I wouldn't wish it on anyone. The key is gone, gone, gone and so is any hope of you getting the cash.

I regret that I didn't know my real mother. Was it Dorinda? She was always looking out for me. I'd like to think it was her, but if not...who cares?

I'll never know either way.

I regret that it'll be a long time before I listen to Gerard Way's music again. By the time you've watched this, he might even have reunited My Chemical Romance. Who knows? I certainly don't.

Finally, I regret that I'll never get a chance to sit my Vocab Test. Honestly, I swotted up and everything. I've used a lot of nice high-scoring words. Words like *obstreperous* and *colloquial* and *melancholy*. Good words that would give me big points.

It doesn't matter anymore.

TCR 02:59:00:00

You're possibly wondering...where *is* Starrsha? Why isn't she here? Where did she go?

By the time you've watched this video, I'll have made my way down to the police station to see my old friend Call Me Clive. Yes, it's tragic but my only friend in the world is a middle-aged policeman. This is what I'm going to do: I'll walk into the police station and I'll ask to see good old Clive. Then he'll see me, soaked in blood but oddly at peace with myself. He'll wonder what happened to me. I'll tell him to send some officers to The Sanctum. They already know the way. I'll tell Clive you're here with my confession.

I'm going to walk into town, that way you'll get a chance to watch this tape.

The police might be outside at the door right now.

As for me...well, I figure prison won't be too bad. My life was spent in jail, trapped within four walls, forced to eat porridge every morning.

I survived that, and I'll survive it again.

Do you think I'll be allowed to sprinkle sugar on my porridge?

TCR 03:00:00:00

<STOP>
<EJECT>

Hello You!

I hope you enjoyed taking a twisted trip through *Glowglass*. With luck you enjoyed it enough that you want to read my other novels – if you haven't already read them, of course.

Conjuring The Infinite is the story of the world's nastiest teenager and his bid to unlock a gateway to another dimension.

Then there's my weirdest book, *Endless Empress,* which one day I might re-title *High School Massacre: The Musical.* It tells the tale of a teenage misfit who masterminds a bombing with the help of a killer unicorn from a fictional country and some equally bizarre friends. I love this book, but it is very strange.

My third novel, *North Of Porter,* is about a teenage boy who takes on a serial killer, despite being armed only with an array of cutting one-liners…and a fake Dolce & Gabbana handbag. (It isn't my life story.)

I'm always touring, so pop along and see the show if I'm nearby then. I always appreciate your support.

Follow me on Instagram: *www.Instagram.com/KirklandCiccone*
Follow me on Twitter: *www.Twitter.com/KirklandCiccone*
Follow me in the blogsphere: *www.KirklandCiccone.com*
But please don't follow me home!

Until next time…